"It's Not the Fact, It's How You React"

by

Andrew O'Donoghue

authorHOUSE®

AuthorHouse™ UK Ltd.
500 Avebury Boulevard
Central Milton Keynes, MK9 2BE
www.authorhouse.co.uk
Phone: 08001974150

First published by AuthorHouse 1/7/2008

ISBN: 978-1-4343-1749-0 (sc)

Printed in the United States of America
Bloomington, Indiana

This book is printed on acid-free paper.

Preface

Andrew O'Donoghue is one of the founding directors and shareholders of Advance Performance, a company whose Mission is to be the first choice provider of corporate and personal development training in the United Kingdom and the United States. He is also a qualified behavioural analyst. Before forming Advance with his two colleagues Mike Finnigan and Heather Wright, he was a solicitor. He left private practice in 1989 to form the legal department in a construction company where he became legal and sales director. He feels extremely fortunate, however, to have found in Advance something about which he is truly passionate – and which has enabled him to banish that "Monday morning" feeling for good!

He is an inspirational speaker and facilitator and has delivered keynote addresses to corporate audiences throughout the United Kingdom, Europe, and the United States. He has developed an outstanding reputation with his clients for combining professionalism with an easy going and accessible style. He specialises now in winning and delivering contracts with large multinational organisations.

He is married to Jacqueline and has one son, Tom. Putting into practice what he preaches, he has embarked with them on the fulfilment of a long-held dream – to move to the United States. Basing his family in Ridgefield, Connecticut, he heads up Advance's U.S. operation. The United Kingdom needn't worry, however, as he returns on a regular basis. The U.S. may be a great place to live, but you just can't get a decent pint of bitter anywhere!

To contact the author or for further information about Advance Performance, email us at inspiration@advance.tv or visit our website: www.advance.tv.

Introduction

"What would you dare to attempt if you knew you were bound to succeed?"

Do you ever ask yourself what stops you from achieving the things in your life that you want? Or why some things come so easy and yet other things, no matter how hard you try, always seem to evade you? Maybe it's a bit like the old school essay question, "What do you want to be when you grow up?" that we probably were all asked. I know that when I used to ask that question of my son, Tom, when he was younger, he would say he wanted to be an astronaut or a scientist or Superman!! Children are great dreamers. What happens then to us? Why is it that all too often the older I get, the lower I set my sights? The nearer become my horizons?

Perhaps that is a sweeping generalisation, but my experience of working with people from different organisations at all levels over the last seven years, whether CEO or Receptionist, Professional Footballer or Security Guard, Lawyer or Filing Clerk, is that everyone has some unfulfilled dreams, desires or goals which they have failed to achieve; not because of a lack of innate talent or ability but because of some other barriers. The aim of this book is threefold: firstly, to get you to identify your own internal barriers; secondly, to identify the source of those barriers; and thirdly, to challenge them giving you a guide as to how they may be removed.

William James one of the first Psychologists claimed:

"Compared to what we ought to be we are only half awake. We make use of only a small part of our physical and mental resources. The human individual lives far within his limits; he possesses powers of various sorts which he habitually fails to use."

Now Mr. James may not have been particularly politically correct but who can argue with his sentiments?

One of my business partners, Michael Finnigan, has published a book entitled *"Mountains and Molehills"*. It is simply a compilation of a dozen or so stories of "ordinary" people like you and me, who attended one of the Advance Performance programmes and who, as a result, have achieved extraordinary things. They have not defied the laws of physics – they are not world famous. They have simply overcome internal barriers to achieve the things that they wanted in their lives.

All of us can do the same. We all have the ability to be a Richard Branson, a Marie Curie, an Einstein, an Evelyn Glennie, a Joe Montana, a Pelé, a Michael Schumacher, or whomever else you care to mention. The temptation is to say, "I'm not as clever as him/her" or "I'm not as talented as him/her". That's just not true. But perhaps I should re-phrase the claim I made above. We can all be great in the roles that we fulfil. We can all be great Leaders, Managers, or Employees. We can all be great Parents, great Sons or Daughters. We can all be great friends. We can all be great "any ones". Therefore, I probably need to clarify exactly what I mean. We all have the ability to be *the best version of ourselves that we choose to be*. Let me repeat that sentence; we <u>all</u> have the ability within us to be the best version of ourselves that we choose to be. We just don't always know how. My aim is to see if I can start to show you.

Throughout the course of this book, you will read stories of talented and successful people. Some will be famous and some you will never have heard of before. You will understand where your abilities come from. You will understand where your talents come from. Why exactly you do the things you do. Why exactly you respond in the way you respond. I'll be asking you to think about how you react in different situations.

For instance, what are you like when you wake up on a Monday morning? Imagine – it's November 1st, 6:00 a.m. and you look out of the window. It's raining and you've got to go to work. What is the first thought that enters your head? Is it something like, "World, leave me alone?" What do you want to do? Just go back to bed? Do you wish it was Saturday or Sunday? Have you ever gone back to bed "just for 5 minutes" – just for those few extra seconds of warmth and comfort that allow you to put off having to deal with what the day is about to throw at you?

Or have you ever woken up *thinking* it was a Saturday, sighed, smiled, and turned over just as the alarm goes off…*on Friday morning??* Well, I'm sure lots of us have been there.

Yet Mondays don't seem to affect everyone that way. There are some people who seem to be able to deal with them much better than others. Why? We've all had that feeling haven't we? You get up, it's raining, you go out, you stand in the puddle, your shoes get wet, and the whole tone of the day is set. Based on what? Well apparently it's based upon the weather. On that basis, therefore, England is a very unfortunate place to live - trust me! And yet if you live in Washington State or Oregon I can imagine what is going through your head right now!!

What happens when you wake up on the 1st July, the sun is shining, you're in the middle of a heat wave, and you have to get on the bus to go to work, or you're on the train, or you're on the subway, and you go to the office that doesn't have air conditioning? I bet the same people that respond with a sigh and a groan to the bad weather respond with a sigh and a groan to the good weather. Perverse isn't it?

Throughout this book, you will understand and see why you do that; why you respond in different ways to different situations; and why the simplest things can affect the way you behave, the way you perform, the way you act, even when that kind of behaviour is the last thing that you want to happen. You will also see why different people respond in different ways to the *same* situation.

My colleagues and I at Advance specialise in performance improvement in individuals, teams, and organisations. One of the most common barriers to people and organisations achieving the things that they want to achieve, in our experience, seems to be people's inability or lack of desire to deal with change. It is probably the most common thing we are asked to address.

Fundamentally people are creatures of habit. The maxim "I know what I like, and I like what I know" is commonplace. We have people on programmes harking back to "the good old days", berating "the management" for forcing them to go through change. One organisation that has been a client for some years had people 6 years ago wanting to return to those good old days. Six years later there are people still making the same request. The only issue is that those good old days now being referred to are the ones which were being complained about six years ago.

The cold hard fact is that change is inevitable. It happens as sure as night follows morning. If our response is that we are not going to like change or that the experience will be painful, we should not be surprised if that is the result that we get.

You may have picked up other books like this, maybe looking for an answer in the past, maybe just out of curiosity. This may, however, be the first time that you've picked up a book on personal development, or the psychology of success, or whatever heading you find this book under in the library or in the bookshop. Whichever it is, I would like you to make yourself a promise. Finish the book! It isn't a long book and is (I hope) an easy read. I'm not going to blind you with science. When I present this book in lecture format or as part of an Advance Performance Programme people often feel that they already know what I am saying and that I'm telling them nothing new. Well neither I nor any of my colleagues at Advance have ever claimed to be gurus. I would suggest to you that all of the material to be found in all of the two and a half million plus titles in this area of writing, contain thinking which has been around for centuries. Marcus Aurelius, the 2nd Century Roman Emperor was a great writer, thinker and philosopher and once wrote:

"If something ails or bothers you it's not the thing itself, but the importance you attach to it; and that (i.e. the importance that you attach to it) *you have the power to change at any time."*

Well, isn't that the case with most things in life? But isn't it equally the case that we so often miss the blindingly obvious until someone gives us a wake–up call? In fact, that's exactly how one delegate on a programme some years ago described his feelings after he saw what you are about to read. He said that he felt like someone had slapped him in the face and issued him with a wake–up call. Maybe you will feel like you have received a metaphorical "slapping" and if that is the case I make no apology.

Even if you do feel like you have been slapped I know you'll enjoy the book. You'll have fun. You'll hear lots of stories about lots of ordinary people who are successful *as they define it*. You have the same ability and capability within you.

CHAPTER 1 – "If I Can Do It, Why Can't You?"

I wonder how many textbooks there are in the world. I wonder how many lessons, lectures, and seminars are given each week to how many millions of people throughout the world. All to what end? Well, people want to learn. Maybe they want to learn French or German, or they want to learn algebra or how to cook, or applied mathematics or applied physics. I suppose some people have learning "thrust" upon them (if you have children, just ask them!!). I wish I had a pound or a dollar for every time someone told us that they had been "sent" on an Advance programme.

My suggestion is (and it doesn't matter what the subject, what the topic of the book) that the purpose is the same. The purpose of any training is to change behaviour.

On first thinking about it, this may not seem to be the case. But look at it this way. In learning French, we want to become a person who speaks French – a person who behaves differently. In learning applied mathematics, I suppose you want to become a mathematician. The point I'm getting at is that the majority of textbooks and lessons are there to teach skills – skills that we don't otherwise possess. Or perhaps it would be more accurate to say skills that we don't think we would otherwise possess.

Take any classroom in any country in the world. You will find some wonderfully talented teachers delivering exciting lessons on any topic you could think of, say in a room of 30 pupils. Will all those pupils leave at the end of the year with the same results, with the same ability to apply the lessons learned? The answer is, "Of course not." But why is that? Well, the obvious answer is that each pupil will have different talents and abilities. Some people are 'naturally' good at maths. Some people are 'naturally' good at languages, aren't they? If I am not one of those people, then it may well be that all the teaching in the world, all the lessons in the world, all the textbooks in the world aren't going to help me. What would happen, however, if I were to be abandoned in the middle of a foreign country unable to leave and unable to speak the language? I wonder how quickly I would become "good" at that language.

Heather, one of my business partners, has a brother who, at the time of writing this book, lives in Italy. She says that at school he was "no good at languages", yet now his telephone answering machine sounds like a translation tape from a United Nations debate. He lived first in France and then Italy and, of course, picked up both languages fluently, because he **had to**. I wonder how many other things you and I could do if we "had to".

How many of you at this moment are thinking of subjects at school – things that you were good at, things that you weren't good at. For the things that you weren't good at, the teaching didn't help did it? Let's see if we can discover why.

Take a look at this picture of a tree.

I think the first things that your eyes are drawn to are the leaves – the foliage. What are the first things people notice about you? Well, psychologists tell us that it's your "foliage" i.e. your behaviour. It's the things you say and the things you do. It's our body language, the way we speak, the way we dress, the way we laugh. It's how you respond in different situations. The things you can do; the things you can't do – all of which are shown at the surface level by the way you act and behave.

I'm going to tell you something now, maybe that you already knew, but if you didn't, this is going to get you really thinking the next time you go to a dinner party or go out to a restaurant or bar. Psychologists also tell us that we make first impressions of people that we meet for the first time based upon the first 15 seconds of meeting them. The first 15 seconds! Now, when you go to that party, meeting people for the first time, who do they see? Am I the only one who puts on a front? I very much suspect not. So often when we go into new situations, we behave in a way that we think will get us accepted or liked or respected, or whatever is appropriate to that group of people in that situation. If I go for a job interview the chances are that I will try to show the interviewer the person that I think he or she wants to see – and that isn't always the real me.

Think of the last time that you actually attended an interview. If you have ever been to an interview skills class one of the things you are often told is simply to "be yourself". Sometimes, however, I believe that people think that the interviewer may be looking for something different than "myself" and, therefore, compensate accordingly. This is one of the things that can make the interviewing process so challenging.

Now, if I'm doing that to you, you are all doing that to me! And I am basing my first impressions of you on that. Not the *real* you. Not the deep down you, not the true you – but rather the person that you choose to show me. I see your foliage. I see the things that you say and the things that you do.

What you should do now is turn back to the picture of the tree. In the middle, at the top, in the space just above the leaves, write the words, 'Behaviour/Performance/Results', and just on the leaves underneath write the words, 'The Things I Say and Do'. The model of the tree will form the perfect analogy as we go through the book to indicate why people do the things they do and why there are many people who find change difficult to accept and sustain.

On the right hand side, write the word 'Best' or 'Peak' (or both) and underneath those words, write 3 or 4 of your own words that you would use to describe you when you are at your absolute 100% best. What would I see in you? How do you think others might describe you? What behaviours would I see? Once you have done that I would just like you to pause for a second and think about something. The question I asked is, "What are *you* like at *your* best?" I do not see it as my role to tell you what that should be. I believe that would be arrogant of me in the extreme. I don't know you and have never met you so how can I in all sincerity tell you how to be. That is your definition and your choice.

I have seen words appear on people's lists like buzzing, being hyper, outstanding, awesome and unstoppable. When that happens in a programme you can sometimes almost see people visibly shrink because you know that they are thinking,

"I could never possibly be like that." The crucial point for me here is – that's okay!! You don't have to be like anyone else!! It really is okay to be you.

I once heard a speaker say to a large audience that we could "all be perfect" – like he was!!! When I heard him say that, two things came into my head. Firstly, I didn't believe that I could be "perfect" like him (he must have been about 6'4", ruggedly handsome, and chiselled out of granite!), and anyway I didn't believe (and still don't) that perfection exists. And, secondly, and more importantly, I didn't want to be like him. I simply wanted to be (and still do want to be) *a better version of me*. Surely that's all that any of us could ask for. I once had a boss who told me that one of my "problems" was that I needed to be more "like him"!! Perhaps at the time I did need to change in some way – but not in a way to make me more like him. Maybe what I needed to do was to simply be a *better me*!

If you have written words down, therefore, such as calm, in control, relaxed, analytical or quiet, then that's okay, too. The point of this exercise is to ask you to describe you at your best. I believe it would be totally wrong of me, therefore, to print any words on the tree in your copy of this book. I cannot tell you what 'best' is for you. I know what it is for me and that's about it.

Now, on the left hand side of the tree I would like you to undertake a similar exercise, but this time write the word 'Worst'. Underneath that word, write the words that describe you when you are at your absolute worst. I am not going to give any suggestions here – people can usually manage this task quite easily on their own. Once you have done this look at the words you've written. Then ask yourself a couple of questions:

The first question is this:

On which side of the tree would I like to spend my time?

I would hope that the answer is fairly simple. We all surely want to be on the right hand side as opposed to the left. I realise, however, that this is not going to be achievable all the time (unless you are like the speaker I mentioned before). Most of us are human and the realities of life mean that we all naturally fluctuate. Perhaps we don't fluctuate between extremes but we certainly fluctuate. I have only ever had one person disagree with me on that. He said that he was always right down the middle never moving more than a few degrees either way. Who am I to judge, but that sounds like an extremely mundane existence to me.

Remember the question is one of choice. Where would you choose to be if you could? I have only ever had two people say that they would choose to be on the left. One said that he liked being on the left because he enjoyed being miserable! A real joke or humour used to defuse a sense of unease? You decide! In fairness, I think he was probably just having a bit of fun. Yet it does seem that many of us find it easier to pick up our own faults and negatives rather than look at the positives.

The second person, however, was a little more serious. He tried to argue that he would on occasion actively choose to be at his worst. I must confess that I am not often lost for words but on this occasion I was completely bemused. I thought that perhaps I had not explained myself properly – in all honesty, I think I was trying to get him out of a hole since one of his managers was also in the room. He assured me, however, that he did actively choose on occasions to be at his worst – a fact which was confirmed with a vigorous nod of the head by one of his colleagues!

Well, apparently the story of this man's admission spread like wildfire through the organisation and I'm afraid, sadly for him, within six months he had lost his job. I think perhaps that they had taken a look at his CV/resumé and decided that he had got his job under false pretences. (If you don't believe me, take a look at your own CV or resumé and tell me where it says that at times you are going to choose to be at your worst. I haven't found one yet! But more of that in a minute).

In this context though, I think I should also mention that there is almost certainly a case to be argued for "appropriate best behaviour." It may not always be appropriate to be buzzing or energetic. Sometimes calmness, empathy, or sympathy could be the order of the day depending upon the situations in which we find ourselves. This re-emphasises the need, as far as I am concerned, for you to understand what "best" means for you. I will openly say that on occasions me being at my best means relaxing on the sofa with a beer in my hand watching sport (although I am sure that my wife Jacqui may not always agree with this!).

The second question I have to ask is this:

On a scale of 0 to 100, when 0 measures you at your absolute worst and 100 is a measure of you at your absolute best, what percentage of your life to date have you spent being at your 100% absolute best as you define it? How often have you actually been at 100?

This is a really interesting one. When we ask this type of question at seminars and programmes we deliver, it's fascinating to see people's responses. You do get some people who genuinely say that they believe that they live their lives at their absolute best (at 100) 70–80% of the time. What a great place to be. When people give that kind of response, however, you can also see other people shake their heads in disbelief. One thing that I would ask you to remember though is that the question was, "How often do you spend life at 100%"? It wasn't, "How often are you above 50?" or even "How often are you at 99?" We are talking, I suppose, about "perfection". With this in mind, therefore, we often also get the answer, "Never." People will ask how can you define 100 or even how can you put a measure on best. If you really think about it there is a valid point here. I remember the feeling I had on my wedding day, and how it was the first second that I set eyes on my son as a baby, and the first time I stood in front of an audience and received a standing ovation. All these things were as close to 100 as I could imagine. These occasions can be, however, few and far between, and so I can see why people might think that way.

To put all your minds at rest though, the average answer we receive from people from all walks of life, from all jobs, professions across the entire spectrum, is between 2–5% – probably nearer to 2% than 5%. And please remember that we have worked with elite athletes, household names at the top of their respective sports, and the realisation soon dawns that they are no different than you or me. They are still

9

striving to be better versions of themselves; it is perhaps just that the measures are different.

Okay, so some of you can now breathe a sigh of relief.

But…I do have one final question that I would like you to answer. Now I am not saying that people necessarily do this, but if you were to get up in a morning and aim for something in terms of behaviour or performance on a scale of 1 to 100…

What would you aim for?

50? 60? 70? More? Or is a better question…

What should you aim for?

I really hope that the answer "100" has sprung straight into your head. I remember vividly, however, a lady in one of my classes (when I said that you should aim for 100) saying that she aimed for 50 every day because 100 (perfection in her eyes) didn't exist. Now I have already agreed with her on that – but her second reason for aiming for only 50 was that she was never likely to be disappointed!!! To be honest, I felt almost sad at this point. Imagine not aiming for something you want because of the fear of disappointment if you fail? I think there's a whole other book on that subject!

But back to her first reason – you shouldn't aim for 100 because perfection doesn't exist. Perhaps I should explain myself and clarify exactly what I mean (as I did on that day to the lady in question.) My point is this – in terms of aiming for something, it is my deepest belief that everyone, every day should aim for 100 – i.e., aim to be…

The best version of themselves that they can be on that day given the circumstances that they face.

You see, I think that lots of people have the right to demand it of you. I think that the organisations that you work for have the right to expect it and demand it of you. They have the right to expect you to come to work on a daily basis and give it your best shot – be the best you that you can be on that given day within the given circumstances that you find yourself in at that particular time. That doesn't mean that one day you may not be better than on another. It just means that we should give it the best we can in any given situation.

One of the reasons I say this is that if I asked you right now to take a look at your CV's or resumés that I mentioned earlier I absolutely guarantee that they would say that that is what you do every day (or words to that effect), and any prospective employer can expect you to do that if they will only give you a chance by giving you a job. I have never yet seen a CV that says, "Not good on a Monday morning," or "On a Friday afternoon I tend to wind down for the weekend," or "The week before holiday/vacation time I become demob happy and you won't get much out of me!" We just don't do that and, therefore, I think our companies/organisations have the right to expect that we will be the best us that we can be each day.

I absolutely guarantee that you all find yourselves frequently in situations where you demand that other people aim for 100. For instance, imagine yourself the next time you are on a plane going on vacation or on a business trip. The Captain comes over the PA system to give the usual pre-flight briefing which is delivered something like this...

"Good morning everyone, this is Captain Bob Clarkson speaking. Today's flight time into JFK will be 7 hours 20 minutes and we shall be cruising at a height of 35,000 feet. We shall be departing over Liverpool and crossing the Irish coast over Dublin, leaving around Shannon. We shall then make our way across the Atlantic reaching the Eastern seaboard of the United States around the area of Maine, flying over Boston, Cape Cod, Long Island, and into Kennedy. We are expecting a relatively smooth crossing, but I would ask you to keep your seat belts loosely fastened when in your seats in case of unexpected clear air turbulence. I feel that I owe it to you to warn you that really it would have been better if you had flown with me last week!! You see I'm not feeling too good this morning – I had a few drinks last night and I'm tired and have a headache and my hands are a little unsteady. Everything will probably be fine so I don't want you to worry. I'm sure you understand though that it's just not reasonable for you to expect me to be at my best all the time!!"

Am I the only one who just decided to take the QE II?? Or imagine just before you go into the operating theatre seeing the surgeon with bloodshot eyes and shaking hands saying, "I'm sure everything will be fine, it usually is. I haven't lost one yet!!"

Okay, so this is a little exaggerated, but I hope you get my point. I also think that there are lots of others who expect us to be aiming to be the best we can be. What about:

- ➤ Friends
- ➤ Husbands
- ➤ Wives
- ➤ Partners
- ➤ Sons
- ➤ Daughters

Don't they have the right to expect you to give it your best shot in lots of circumstances?

But actually, I think that there is someone who has the right to expect you to aim to be the best that you can be on a daily basis more than the rest put together. And that person is of course – YOU? I think that if we don't aim to give it our best shot in any given situation – be the best version of ourselves that we can be at that time – then quite frankly we are selling ourselves short, and I think that's a real pity.

So typically, what do people do about this? What do we do when we want to get more out of ourselves? Well, I think I've already given the answer to that – we try to develop new skills. We go on courses. We read books. We look for help from all kinds of sources. Often though, all of the things we look to do are aimed at changing our behaviour, changing who we are at this surface level. In other words, if you were that tree in the picture and had brown leaves and you wanted to change them to green ones, you often seek to develop new skills to make them green. Too often though, the skills we acquire are as painters and decorators!!! We paint the leaves green. We force a change in behaviour. I think I said a little earlier that sometimes people put on a front. So, we don't make any permanent change.

However, I was told a story some time ago by an ex British Army Lieutenant Colonel who I thought was joking when he said that this is exactly what the army does when a dignitary or royalty visit the barracks. Apparently the army paints everything. The army paints the walls white, the coals black and, believe it or not, the grass green! Well, painting the grass green might be okay for when Her Majesty visits army barracks. But what happens to us if we do that? What happens if you paint your leaves green? You don't have to be an arboriculturist to know that, at best, after a while the paint will crack, flake, and fall off. The original colour of the leaves – those brown leaves that you were trying to get rid of – will come through, just as if they'd never been painted in the first place. We are exactly the same. I know plenty of people, and I'm sure you do too, who simply put on the front that I described before. They paint their leaves so that people see only the behaviour that they want them to see. Not the real them. Anyone who has ever done this will know that this is difficult to sustain. It's not easy to keep on being someone you're not and eventually you revert to type.

If you are shy, try being an extrovert for long periods of time. If you are assertive try taking a back seat and be compliant. If you are fast-paced and like to show urgency, try being calm and unemotional. You may be able to make changes for short periods, but I challenge you to sustain those changes.

There is, of course, another scenario with painting leaves. In the worst cases, painting the leaves can kill them – and ultimately the tree itself. If you are not particularly good at something or if there is something about you or in your life that you do not like, you should not be surprised if going on a course or reading a textbook does nothing other than make a temporary change. We all tend to revert to type eventually.

And yet I feel I have spent half my life being told "how" to behave. I don't necessarily mean that as it may at first sound. Certainly as a child I was always being told what to do or how to behave – most of us probably were. Some things I found extremely easy, particularly if I enjoyed the thing I was being asked to do or if I was particularly good at it (and, surprise, surprise, the two often coincided!).

Other things, however, I found extremely difficult – and I don't just mean as a child. I remember when I was a lot younger in previous employment, I was sent on a time management course by a former boss because he said, "O'Donoghue, you are the worst time manager in this office." And, of course, he was right. So I went on the course. It was an excellent course delivered by one of the market leaders in the area. Did it work for me? Well, if I were to write words in terms of my time management skills on the model of the tree just as I've asked you to do, the words would have appeared on the left hand side and would probably have read, 'lousy time manager'. That was me. That was the colour of my leaves. Giving me a time management course did nothing other than temporarily change the colour of my leaves. In my case, the change lasted for about 5 minutes because when I got back to the office, the first place I put the time management folder was in the bottom drawer of my desk. I did nothing to implement changes. This wasn't because there was anything wrong with the course. I've already said it was delivered by one of the market leaders and was an excellent course. The trouble was I was a lousy time manager. Giving me all the skills in the world made no difference as long as I *saw* myself as a lousy time manager. I didn't use the manual, I didn't open the manual, I didn't use the lessons I was taught – because I didn't have the time!! That's what poor time managers have very little of. It's exactly the same with you. I'll bet many of you have been sent off to sales courses or customer service courses and come back no different. You have the manual, just not the incentive or desire to make permanent change and use the tools.

Have a look at the tree. The leaves don't just sit there floating on air. The leaves are there because they grow out of the branches and in terms of you, it's exactly the same. The way you behave, the way you act in any given situation is dictated directly by the way you FEEL about that situation.

CHAPTER 2 – "I Did It Because I Felt Like Doing It"

On the next page, we have another diagram of the tree. Go back to the original tree in Chapter 1, and copy the words you wrote there onto the new diagram. Then, in between the two lines – where the branches are, write the words, 'Feelings and Emotions'. The way you feel – your emotions about any given situation – will *always* tend to dictate the way you behave or the way you act or the way you perform.

Do the same exercise then as you did previously. On the right hand side of the diagram, in the branches, underneath the words you have written for you at your absolute best, write the words that you would use to describe you when you feel fantastic; when you feel outstanding. I'll bet a number of these words will correspond with the words you've already written above – buzzing, tremendous, terrific, wonderful, happy, etc., etc. Then do the same on the left hand side of the tree. Under worst performance, again in the branches, write your negative feelings; write the lousy feelings; write the words that describe how you feel when you do get up in the morning (if you are that kind of person) and look out of the window and its cold and wet, and you've got to go to work...

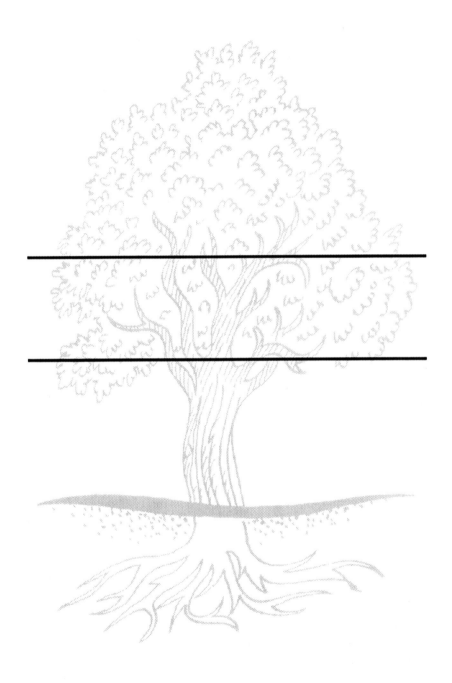

Now, you don't need me to tell you, you don't need a teacher or a psychologist to tell you, that if you wake up in a morning feeling the way that you have described yourself on the right hand side of that model, then that is far more likely to produce you at your best than if you wake up feeling how you've described yourself on the left hand side. Obvious isn't it? But you also know that there are times when you can be feeling the way you described on the right and suddenly something happens, something inconsequential and insignificant that can take you immediately from right to left and ruin your day.

Let me give you an example. For those of you who are married, imagine you've been working really hard all week. You've been going in early, coming home late, because perhaps you've had a deadline to meet, and all week you've been looking forward to the weekend. For those of you with children, you've arranged for them to stay with friends and you're looking forward to a quiet, relaxing weekend with your wife/husband/partner, and that's what has been driving you on all week. You finish work on Friday and drive home, looking forward to that first gin and tonic or that first glass of wine or that martini, to a nice relaxing dinner at home, or maybe you have planned to go out to dinner, just the two of you. Maybe you are just looking forward to generally putting your feet up, relaxing, and chilling out. You walk through the front door and you are greeted by your husband/wife/partner with those immortal words, "Darling, great news for you. Mother's staying for the weekend!"

Now before all of those of you who are mothers-in-law put the book down, and particularly before my own mother-in-law strangles me, I know that's just a stand up comedian's joke, but I think you get my message. The slightest things can change the way we feel, and when we change the way we feel, those feelings often affect the way we behave or perform.

Another phenomenon that this often gets me thinking about is that of road rage. If ever there was a perfect example of situations where people can be feeling great and suddenly something happens to make them feel awful and affect the way they behave or perform, even to the extent that it affects who they are, then road rage would be one.

I remember some time ago I had a delegate attend a course who, when I mentioned road rage, looked at me and said, "They've told you about me, haven't they?" The rest of the group fell about laughing. I assured the delegate I knew absolutely nothing about him and he proceeded to tell us a story.

He had previously described himself as having the 'best job in the world'. He said he looked forward to getting up every morning. He never had Monday morning blues. He told the group that one warm summer's day, he was driving down the M6 Motorway heading south towards London from the North. He said he hadn't a care in the world. He was going to his job, a job he loved; the sun was shining, it was warm, and things were great. He said he was in the inside lane of the motorway when a 'boy racer' (his words not mine) came from the outside lane across to the middle lane, across the inside lane and up the exit ramp, just narrowly missing the front of his vehicle and causing him to brake suddenly to avoid a collision (although in retrospect he felt he probably over-reacted even at that stage).

He then went on to describe the most remarkable change. He said he immediately changed from feeling great to feeling angry – 'road rage'. He said to himself, "'I'll have you" (actually those weren't the words he used; the ones he did use are certainly not printable in this book!). He described how he then followed this 'boy racer' up the exit ramp and round the roundabout at the top. He said that he and the driver in front exchanged pleasantries, using the traditional hand gestures so common between motorists!! He said that he followed this driver for about ½ mile down a dual carriageway, until the driver in front pulled into a lay-by/parking area. He said he thought this was his chance. He pulled in behind him, screeching to a halt, throwing the door open and running up to the car in front. He described how, as he reached the rear of the other vehicle, he heard and saw the wheels spin, and the driver crossed this side of the dual carriageway directly in front of on-coming traffic, bumped across the central reservation and headed back in the direction from which he'd come.

The delegate then said that he thought to himself, "This time I'll really have you" (again, the words have been changed to protect the innocent!). He did the same. He went across the central reservation and again followed the vehicle. He said, however, that this time he 'played clever' and hung back, staying behind a small van about 6 or 7 vehicles behind the other driver. He then proceeded to follow him – follow him for approximately 4 miles!! So, bear in mind, this individual had been heading south towards London, not a care in the world going to the job he loved. Something had happened (well, you might even think that something had not happened – have you ever come across people who will go to great lengths to tell you how upset they are about things that *nearly*

21

happened? Think about it for a moment). So something had happened that changed the way he felt from great to one of rage and had caused him now to travel 4 miles towards Stoke, completely out of his way.

So, after about 4 miles, the car in front pulled into a petrol station. He spied his opportunity and pulled in behind the car. This time, however, the driver hadn't seen him. He ran out of the car and up to the other driver's car. The window was down – it was a hot day. He described how he put his right hand through the window and grabbed the throat of this... 65 year old 'boy racer'! He said the driver was 'a little, grey-haired old man'. Now, obviously this man panicked, hit the electric window button and the window started to rise. My delegate said that any sensible man would, of course, immediately have let go, but not him. Instead of letting go of the man's throat as the window came up he punched it with his left hand, shattering the glass and cutting his knuckles. It was only this event that brought him to his senses. He went back to his car, got in and quietly drove off. (He said, "I even think I said, 'Sorry'").

Now, that may be an extreme example, but how often do we let the little things affect us? You see it at work when monthly or quarterly figures are produced that aren't in line with projections. If the boss is angry then it can affect the entire atmosphere of the office – the way the office feels and, therefore, affects the way the people in it work.

My colleague, Heather, once had a delegate on a programme who very openly and honestly said that one of the things he wanted was to change his demeanour, so that the way he felt and behaved did not have a knock on effect with the people within his office. He described how his secretary used to bring him a cup of coffee in the morning. By simply looking at him she said that she could determine just how he was feeling and, therefore, just how he would *be* for the rest of the day. Based on that, she said that she used to go to the other members of the team with either thumbs up or thumbs down (à la Gladiator arena)! If it was thumbs down, you can bet that it was then a 'thumbs down' day for the rest of the people in that office. He wanted to change that. He recognised the powerful effect he could have either positively or negatively on the feelings of the people with whom he worked, and by definition, therefore, on the performance of the people he worked with, simply by his own demeanour.

I remember working in an organisation where at holiday time you always tried to get the holiday list immediately after the boss had selected his holidays in the hope that you could select either the two weeks before his holidays or the two weeks after. In this way you would have an entire four week period (almost one twelfth of the year) where you didn't have to deal with him. Unfortunately, the more junior you were, the lower down in the pecking order you came, and people would be almost depressed if they found that they could only have the same two weeks as him!!

Also when the time came for the boss to take his two week break, it was party time in the office. The atmosphere would be lifted. People would arrive in work early. That first week was always the best. The atmosphere changed and more work seemed to get done. But I remember best the feeling of all was waking up on the Monday of the second week knowing that he *still* wasn't going to be around for another week. I know that this sounds pretty sad but perhaps some

23

of you can relate to it. However, at around lunchtime on that second Monday there always seemed to be someone in the office who would look at his or her watch and come out with the immortal line:

"This time next week...he'll be back!"

Immediately you could feel the atmosphere of the entire place sink. In other words, the boss could make us feel bad and he wasn't even there!! I'm not sure that even he realised he was that good!!

If I was to say to you, however, "So the answer is simple, change the way you feel and that, in turn, will change your behaviour or performance" – that's about as real as painting your leaves. I know that different people in different countries respond differently to the same situations. There are certain instances where it is possible to generalise. In our culture in Britain, it just isn't the done thing to show feelings and emotions. We tend to bottle them up.

Try this little exercise. Get a bottle of a carbonated soft drink or carbonated water and play through one of your days next week, maybe tomorrow. Every time you have a feeling or a thought which you would put on the left hand side of your tree, shake the bottle. Say you get up in a morning and it's cold and raining, shake the bottle. If you are a man, perhaps you cut yourself shaving and your wife/partner notices that you have got blood on your collar – shake the bottle. You go to the wardrobe and realise that you don't have a clean shirt ironed – shake the bottle. So you go down and iron a clean shirt. Your son/daughter comes running towards you and gives you a huge hug. The only problem is they've just had toast with jam on, so this time instead of blood, you have jam on your shirt – shake the bottle. You've now ironed the second shirt of the morning and you're late for work. You dash outside and in your hurry you don't notice the puddle that's gathered outside the doorstep, and you step in it. Your shoes, socks, tights, feet are soaking wet – shake the bottle. Because you're 20 minutes later than usual, the traffic is heavier – shake the bottle. You arrive at work and there is an email from your boss saying, "We have a 9 o'clock meeting, where are you?" – shake the bottle. There's a knock on your door, somebody has walked in and treats you disgracefully by asking a terrible question... "How are you?" BANG! Take the top off the bottle. How many times do we take the lid or the cap off the bottle and explode at the wrong person at the wrong time? And what a mess!!

Now some people may think that's good for them – some people like to have controlled explosions. They say it's good, even necessary sometimes to take the top off the bottle – otherwise it may ultimately explode. Well I accept that, but I have a slightly different solution – try this for a week. Try not shaking the bottle up at all!

Constantly shaking that bottle is stressful. It's hard, it's difficult, and while sometimes there is a sense of relief when you have had that explosion, just look at the bottle now. Half its contents have been sprayed all over the carpet. I just hope it isn't blackcurrant juice you used!! (Please read the disclaimer at the front of this book!) Even with a controlled explosion, you still go through the stress initially. I would suggest that it is far, far better not to shake the bottle and not cause yourself that discomfort and stress in the first place. I know that that's easy for me to say! But actually when you examine the scenarios above perhaps it's easier to do than we think. The examples I have been giving all, I suggest fall into two categories:

1. Minor
2. Uncontrollable

The weather, Mondays and traffic are all, I would suggest, relatively minor situations within the bigger scheme of things. There will almost certainly be much bigger events in everyone's life that will be designed to make you shake your bottle. I am simply suggesting that the fewer of the minor things to which we react in that way, the better. Also they are all uncontrollable. As much as we might like to stop traffic/Mondays/rain we just can't.

The realisation that it was extremely important for me to find a way to deal with these kinds of situations came about three years ago as I was driving to a morning presentation. A colleague and I had been asked to present to approximately 50 senior Human Resource Managers and Directors. It was a great selling opportunity for us. The presentation was to start at 9:00 a.m. and was at a venue about a half an hour away from where I lived at the time. Now I hate being late for anything, so I left my home at 7:15 a.m. figuring that even with the worst traffic I would still have plenty of time.

Well I got onto the Motorway and after about 15 minutes of this 30 minute journey, the traffic just stopped. It wasn't that it was moving slowly – it came completely to a standstill. I switched on the radio and found a traffic report that told me that there had been an accident right by the exit I was going to use – 14 miles away. I arrived for my 9:00 a.m.

presentation at 9:50 a.m. Highly impressive!! Fortunately, one of my colleagues was travelling from a different direction and hadn't been caught in the traffic, so he had started without me. When I came to do my part of the presentation I obviously made profuse apologies and explained about the traffic and asked if anyone else had been caught in the snarl-up. About 8 or 10 hands were raised including that of a man who had walked into the room just after me. His tie was twisted, the top button of his shirt was undone, he was sweating, and he was an interesting colour of purple!!

I asked how he felt, and he told me he was embarrassed because he hated being late for anything and knew that the rest of the group would have a laugh at him for walking in in the middle of a speech (which, of course, they had)! I then asked him how he thought I felt. He said that I probably felt the same. But I then asked him to take it a couple of stages further and imagine himself in my position.

> ➢ I was late for my own speech and would be equally embarrassed.
> ➢ People might think I was unprofessional.
> ➢ I was there to sell to this group - if I couldn't even arrive on time for a sales opportunity, what might happen if they actually worked with me.
> ➢ They might tell other people about how unprofessional I was.
> ➢ We were due to do another presentation to another group - perhaps this might be cancelled, etc.

All of that was, of course, true. But what I said to that group was really brought home to me with a vengeance that day. I would much rather be:

➤ Embarrassed
➤ Thought of as unprofessional
➤ Lose business

because I was at the back of a 14 mile traffic queue, than be the poor individual or individuals in the crushed car at the front. Events like that so often put things into perspective. I suppose that what I am saying is that we shouldn't wait for major events to do that – remember Marcus Aurelius – *we* have the power to do that (put things into perspective) at any time.

Before we move on though just take another look at the tree. There is one more scenario that I would like you to consider. How many of you know people who wake up in a morning, or as is more likely, how many of *you* wake up in a morning feeling on the left hand side – feeling down, sad, tired, or drained (and any other words you may have written there) and then, because of the kind of individual you/they are, approach the day in a different way. How many people force themselves to produce the behaviour that they have written down in the top right hand corner? In other words, get up feeling awful or lousy, and try to produce their best.

Yet I think that we often feel that life demands this of us. We are expected to be at our best irrespective of how we actually feel – remember the airline pilot or surgeon? Now I'm not suggesting that it is impossible to do that. Of course, it's possible, people do it every day. My real concern is just how sustainable that kind of approach is in the long-run. If you draw a line across that diagonal from 'awful feelings' through to 'best performance', you might want to write the word 'stress' on that line, because that's what people who are doing that to themselves are putting themselves through. If you are one of those people, just think how that feels. It really isn't a fun place to be is it? And ultimately it isn't good for your health!

So, we have the answer – if you want to be at your best more often, feel at your best more often – in the words of the song:

"Don't Worry, Be Happy!" – Bobby McFerrin

Well, that may be the answer, but have you ever been in a situation where you are feeling really low and someone comes up to you and says something like, "Come on now – pull yourself together. Look on the bright side. Worse things happen at sea!" If those people walk away from you without your giving them a black eye then you are to be commended on your restraint!!! You know as well as I do that switching these things on and off isn't like going up to a tap and turning it on to get a drink because your feelings and emotions don't just appear out of thin air. Have a look at your tree again. Where do your branches, your feelings and emotions, come from? Answer – the trunk of the tree. In terms of the process we're going through now, the trunk of your tree is your 'attitude'.

CHAPTER 3 – "It's Not the Fact, It's How You React!"

Before I say anything more I would like you to do something for me. In the space below I would like you to write down six things to which you have an attitude on a daily basis. When I write the word "attitude" what immediately comes into your head? Just spend a minute now please and write some things down that cause you to have an attitude.

Now take another look at the words that you have written. How many of those words relate to things which cause you to have a positive attitude? Or do a lot of them (or indeed all of them) have a negative connotation for you? You see, the reality is that there are two types of attitude – positive and negative. In my experience, though, if three words are ever likely to produce an instant negative response from the average man or woman in the street, they are the words, "Positive Mental Attitude." I think in many ways we have been immunised or become anaesthetised against "positive thinking" by these words. The concept is often totally misunderstood. Having a positive mental attitude isn't the theory of the philosopher Pangloss in Voltaire's *Candide*, where "all is for the best in the best of all possible worlds". Having a positive mental attitude isn't about painting a smile on your face when the entire world is crumbling around you.

I will never forget my first visit in the 1980's to a well known burger chain restaurant in Wigan in the North West of England. The restaurant had only been open a few weeks and it was here that I encountered John! As I walked in I noticed that the place wasn't that busy, and I could see John from a distance. He looked like he had all the worries of the world on his shoulders. As I got to about six feet away from the counter, however, John's demeanour changed and a smile appeared on his face and he said the immortal words, "Good morning, Sir. Welcome to (insert name of restaurant) Wigan. How may I help you?" A great way to greet a customer, I know, but this really is one of those situations where you had to be there. It was obvious that John didn't want to be! He had quite clearly been told to be positive, to smile when he greeted a customer, and to greet the customer with the 'Company mantra'. Nothing could hide what John was really thinking or feeling. Is that being positive? I don't think so.

I remember watching a documentary on TV some time ago about a school which, the documentary makers said, was a 'positive attitude' school. The children in this school had been taken out of mainstream state education to be taught in an atmosphere of 'positivity'. As a philosophy I support this wholeheartedly. The practice, though, didn't quite match the theory. There was a very interesting little cameo where an 11 year old girl was asked a question by the teacher. The girl gave the correct answer to the question. At the time though she was obviously having a raging attack of pubescent hormones (anyone recognise this?) and looking thoroughly miserable, slumped in the chair avoiding eye contact with the teacher. The teacher at this point hit the desk and shouted, "This is a positive attitude school. I don't care how you feel on the inside as long as you smile on the outside!" Is it any wonder that people have become immunised against this idea if that is their belief as to what being positive is all about. A true positive attitude has nothing to do with painting a smile on your face or punching the air whooping and hollering and giving "high fives". A person who is positive recognises (to slightly amend an American phrase) that "stuff happens". When you have a positive attitude you accept that "stuff happens" and that you have to deal with it – albeit in your own way – but deal with it you must.

On the tree on the previous page, write in the words you had previously written for behaviour and feelings on your other diagrams – so the words you wrote for best and worst behaviour and the words you wrote for great and lousy feelings now appear on this new tree diagram. In the middle of the trunk write the word ATTITUDE. On the right hand side write the word positive, and on the left hand side write the word negative.

We have already shown that we all have attitudes to all sorts of things. Perhaps some of the words you wrote previously for the things to which you have an attitude included things such as 'rude people', 'the job', 'the boss', 'the government', 'the weather' or 'the traffic'. The simple reality is that whatever labels we put on the things to which we have an attitude, we can only ever have an attitude (positive or negative) to one thing – and that is FACTS.

We may call these 'facts' different things as we have already seen – we may call them people; we may call them situations; we may call them circumstances; we may call them "where I live"; we may call them "being unemployed"; we may call them "the job"; we may call them "the boss". The reality is they are all simply facts.

Some people think that facts control them, whilst others think that they have far more control. Either way how people view facts is an external demonstration of their attitude

You see, an attitude is simply a response to facts – it's how people deal with and react to the things that life throws at them on a daily basis. And I would suggest to you that these facts fall into two broad categories, one of which we have already touched upon. These categories are:

1. Controllable
2. Uncontrollable

If you take a look at the things which you wrote down before – those things which cause you to have an attitude – then I suspect that the majority of them will fall into the "uncontrollable" category. If that is the case, then I would like you to think about what you actually do have control over. One thing that absolutely falls into the "controllable" category is our attitude. And as far as your attitude is concerned I have a suggestion to make which at first glance some of you may find startling and some of you may even dismiss entirely; and the suggestion is this –

> The attitude that we take to the facts
> in our lives is a CHOICE.
> And it is a choice – 100% of the time
> – irrespective of the fact.

It isn't a choice some of the time; it isn't a choice most of the time. It is a choice 100% of the time. I suggest that you write the words, 'Attitude to Facts' and '100% Choice' right in the middle of the trunk of the tree.

I recognise that this is quite a big claim to make so I would like to look at some examples and start small to see if I can convince you.

Take the scenario I have already talked about on several occasions of waking up one Monday morning to the pouring rain. If you wake up, look out of the window and let out a sigh, that is simply a negative attitude to a fact – a fact over which you have no control and which you cannot change. Or if you get stuck in that traffic jam and it starts to irritate you, the same applies. We all know that starting a day like that can create a snowball effect leading to you feeling awful about the rest of the day ahead. If you look back to your tree, feeling bad can actually make the day turn out bad. Imagine going to a meeting, or doing a presentation, or going for a job interview, in that state of mind. We all know what the outcome is going to be. In other words, the trunk of that tree – your attitude – supports the branches (your feelings and emotions), and from those branches come the leaves (your behaviour or performance).

Of course, I am generalising here. Not everybody's like that, are they? Imagine that you, being the kind of person you are, go into work that Monday morning when it's been raining but you have had a great weekend and are positive and feeling good. You walk in and you meet the first person in the office who perhaps hasn't quite had the weekend that you have had and maybe isn't quite as up for the day as you are, and you say those immortal words, "Good morning". What response do you get? How do people often respond to those two simple words? Maybe something such as, "Is it?", "What's good about it?" Sometimes you might even just get a grunt. My colleague, Mike, describes a boss that he once worked for who, when Mike used to walk in and say, "Good morning" to him, simply shook his head and stormed off as if to say, "Who is this guy? Doesn't he know how bad things are?"

Then, of course, you being you, make the fatal mistake and ask the one question you should never ask this person first thing on a Monday morning – "How are you?" How do people respond to that question? I issue a challenge to you – for the next week actively listen and record how people respond to the simple question, "How are you?" The responses I have had have varied from things like, "Not so bad", "Can't complain", and "Fine" to "Don't ask?". "What are you on?", "It's Monday!", "I'm having a bad year", "I'm on the crest of a slump" and, one of my favourites, "As good as they'll let me be!!" I would love to know if you can come up with some better ones.

On one occasion Mike and I decided to undertake an impromptu cultural climate survey at one of our new clients. We arrived early for an 8:00 a.m. meeting and were told that we could, if we wished, have breakfast in the staff cafeteria. Never ones to turn down a free breakfast, we headed straight there. While waiting for our bacon and egg to be cooked we stood at the start of the line and Mike, with an over the top positive and cheery, "Good morning," decided to hand out trays to some of the shop floor workers as they came for their breakfast.

You can imagine some of the looks we got, but I think we frightened one particular man more than the rest. As Mike handed him his tray he took one look at these "men in suits", shook his head, and took one large step away from us. Mike, though, wasn't going to be put off. As the man took his breakfast, Mike said to him in an even more effusive manner, "How are you today?" As the man's plate went onto his tray he simply turned to us and said…"Another day nearer retirement!!!"

Mike couldn't resist saying as he walked away, "Do you mind if I ask how old you are?" The reply came back… "35!"

Well, if that is people's attitude to Monday mornings, I have a little secret to share. Monday mornings come round with unerring regularity once a week! Imagine having that kind of attitude to a 'fact' that comes around once per week, just like an express train that can't be stopped.

Incidentally, have you noticed how difficult we English (apologies if you are not English) find it to say, "Yes"? The next time you have some work done at home, ask the person if he or she would like a tea or a coffee. It wouldn't surprise me if the answer that you got was, "I wouldn't say, No!"

Please don't get me wrong though – I'm not saying that I'm perfect. I know exactly how that feels, but for me, I didn't have too much of a problem with Monday mornings. My problem was with Sundays! I hated Sundays (and they still aren't my favourite day of the week)! I used to spend the entire working week looking forward to Fridays. I would finish work on Friday, usually have a very enjoyable Friday night, rested in bed on Saturday (well, before my son, Tom, came along), really enjoyed Saturday, perhaps going out Saturday night and then woke up Sunday morning and .... BANG! Depression. The first thought I used to have when I woke up on a Sunday morning was, "Oh no, it's Monday tomorrow." I've probably wasted several years of Sundays hating them because the day after was Monday. Everything about Sundays used to have a negative connection with me – church bells, going out for drives in the country, afternoon tea, chicken salad, "Skippy the Bush Kangaroo" (now I'm really giving my age away!). Sundays had a different atmosphere about them! Please just think about that for a moment. I know some of you are probably laughing, but I'll bet that the reason a number of you are laughing is that you feel exactly the same.

So often we have a negative attitude to things that we cannot change. As I'm sure you can imagine, in the type of work I do, working with people and teams in organisations from all over the world, one of the 'facts' that often gives rise to a negative attitude in those people is the job they do.

On one occasion in a classroom I had a delegate who had a real challenge with my contention that his attitude was his choice. He told me I was in 'cloud cuckoo land'. He said that it was obvious that I loved my job and that everything in my life was going extremely well. Apparently I didn't understand what he was going through. I didn't work for his company, and I certainly didn't work for his boss. I didn't understand how tough it was in his industry right now, and no matter what, he just didn't agree that he could be anything other than negative about the work situation in which he found himself.

When he finished I told him that I had a foolproof method of solving his situation. I asked for his manager's name. (He was a little suspicious at first but I assured him that I wasn't going to speak to his manager.) I then took a piece of paper and wrote the following which I then handed to the delegate.

> *Dear (Manager):*
>
> *I resign.*
>
> *Yours sincerely,*
>
> *Signed*

I am sure you can imagine the response. I must confess that with hindsight I handled this rather badly and was probably a little too 'in this man's face', because he almost exploded. He said that it was clear that I didn't come from the real world and that things were obviously alright for me. I mustn't have had the same commitments. I mustn't have had the same mortgage, the same electricity bills, or have had to pay for children, clothes, etc. He was married, had a family, a mortgage, credit cards, etc., and I think he finished by saying that I was stupid (or something to that effect!).

Well, of course, I do have all those commitments, but the point that I was trying to make (however clumsily) was that in fact he could have made the decision simply to resign and walk out of his job. Now I accept that he would have been extremely foolish to do so given his commitments, but that doesn't take away from the fact that it is something that theoretically he could have done. Of course, if we are not going to change the facts then I would suggest that it is crucial that we all look to deal with the one thing over which we have complete control – and that is, how we respond to those facts (i.e., our attitude).

In theory, anyone could resign tomorrow but resignation, for the vast majority of people, isn't a reality. But if that's not reality, then I have to learn to accept a few things. I have to learn to accept that where I am today is a direct result of the choices that I have made in my life. One thing is of course certain, I cannot change those choices. I cannot change the past.

A good friend of mine – we'll call him Chris – returned from holiday a few years ago, gave me a call, and asked me out for a beer (I am changing his name for this story because if he recognises himself in this he might become an ex-friend). When I saw him, I commented on how well he looked (he had a great tan and seemed really relaxed.) Naturally I asked him how his holiday had been. The first words out of his mouth were, "It was too hot." Now he had been to Corfu in August! He clearly hadn't gone there for the skiing!! I said, though, that I loved going to places like Spain and Greece because of the fantastic variety of restaurants and the ability to eat outside. He said that really he didn't enjoy foreign food and couldn't wait to get home for sausage, egg and chips! I know you could accuse me of being an old cynic, but he could have gone to any English seaside resort and have been guaranteed no sun and have been able to eat fish and chips to his hearts content. Why do so many people seem hell bent on looking for the negative in everything?

It's time for me to be completely honest with you. I used to spend a lot of my life living on the left hand side of that tree – and at times I still do. Perfect, I'm not. I had a nickname in my previous job – "Hatchet Jack". Now Hatchet Jack thought that he was a pretty okay kind of guy. But the Hatchet Jack nickname came from the people who worked for him. It had something to do with the number of people he had fired in his previous life. Maybe he had got it wrong? But surely that was just Hatchet Jack at work.

Well, when he talked to his friends, though, he found out that he could be Hatchet Jack as a friend. He actually found out that when he behaved in that way he made sure that his friends knew about it and that they felt the same way as he did. That came as an interesting revelation. Have you ever met anyone who thought that they could be a complete S.O.B. at work and yet somehow change when they left work?

The biggest revelation came, however, when he spoke to his wife. She told him that although he wasn't like that all of the time he could certainly be Hatchet Jack as a husband and perhaps worst of all to the 7 year-old son who, he told anyone and everyone that would listen, was the light of his life! Now that really hurt!

I apologise for writing that little section in the third person but it still hurts to think about it! I have had people say to me, "Why is it not okay to be Hatchet Jack at work? Why should I be positive? Why should I contribute? What did they ever do for me?" The best answer to that question comes not from me but from Nelson Mandela. Mandela was interviewed after spending 27 plus years in prison. He was asked if he was bitter. His answer, in my opinion, should be compulsory learning in every school in every country of the world, because he said:

"I would love to be, but I haven't got the time. I have learned that you cannot do wrong in one area of your life and expect to do right in others."

In other words, I couldn't expect to be Hatchet Jack at work while at the same time be a great friend, loving husband, and father outside work. It just doesn't happen that way. But the biggest reality that came home when I first started to do the work that I do now is that the one person, who suffered more than anyone else when I was Hatchet Jack, was me. How ridiculous is that?

We are really fortunate at Advance because due to our line of work we meet some fascinating people. We also meet some famous people. If you have heard of us before it is likely to be in connection with the work we do in elite sport. This started in 1998 with snooker legend, Jimmy White. After working with my colleague, Mike, and me for a couple of months, Jimmy beat the then world number 1, Stephen Hendry, in the first round of the World Championships at The Crucible Sheffield – something he hadn't done in 14 previous attempts. As a result of Jimmy going public and giving us a lot of the credit for his success (we were in over 30 press articles and TV interviews, and the final chapter of Jimmy's autobiography, *"Behind the White Ball"* is about the work we did), our involvement in sport has become widespread and an integral part of our business strategy.

At the time of going to press we have worked with:

- ➢ European Tour and Ryder Cup winning professional golfers
- ➢ Two Premiership Rugby League teams (Wigan and Hull)
- ➢ The South African National Cricket Team, the Sri Lankan National Cricket Team and Lancashire County Cricket Club
- ➢ We have acted as advisers to the West Indies Cricket Board
- ➢ Bolton Wanderers Football Club for 4½ years
- ➢ Everton Football Club (ongoing)

We have also been fortunate enough to work with one of the most inspirational men that I know – the captain of an England football team. However, I know that I have probably lost about half of you right now because you are turning to the front of the book looking at when it was written to see if you can work out who I am talking about.

This man also holds the junior British record for the 100 metres. He holds the world land speed record. He holds two World Formula Two speedboat records. He holds a record for flying a plane around the coastline of the U.K., and at the time of writing this, he is preparing to fly a helicopter around the coastline of the U.K. His future plans include flying a plane across the Atlantic and taking a group of disabled people (together with Sir Rannulph Fiennes) to the North Pole.

Now you are probably really confused (although I may have given you a little clue in the proposed trek to the North Pole). In case you haven't guessed yet (and just to confuse you even more, most of the football aficionados among you won't have even heard of him), the man I am talking about is a man named, Steve Cunningham. We were fortunate enough to meet Steve towards the end of 1999 and I have to say he is one of the nicest, funniest and certainly the single most inspirational man it has been my pleasure to meet. You see Steve was captain of the blind England Football Team. He holds the junior record still for 100 metres for a blind athlete. He holds the world land speed record over a standing mile for a blind athlete – an average speed of just under 150 miles per hour with a top speed of over 173 miles per hour. In the summer of 2000, he broke two Formula Two speedboat world records. Steve is unassuming and likeable. The first time I met him he spoke to a group of ours one Saturday morning. He talked about his life. How he was fully sighted until he was eight and how from the age of eight he gradually lost his sight until, by the age of 13, he was completely blind.

Whenever I have met him he has only ever been happy, laughing, and enjoying himself. One of the members of the group he came to address asked him whether or not he was always like that – whether he was always so positive and upbeat. His answer was simple – "Of course not, I'm human aren't I?" He described how he does, from time to time, feel low and depressed, particularly when he thinks about his beautiful wife and his two beautiful daughters who he will never see. But then he says to himself, "What am I going to do?" He knows better than anyone else that I have met that he has a choice. He has a "fact" in his life which he (in his own words) "absolutely cannot change." He has had both his eyes surgically removed. Based upon that fact he has choices to make. If he chose to spend his life on the left hand side of your tree diagram under that word negative, then he would spend his life perhaps with the kind of feelings that you have written down which can only lead to one thing. And he doesn't want that for himself, his family, or any of the other people around him. I very much suspect that neither do you.

It is really important to understand something else. I was with Steve at a Corporate Event some months ago – I was facilitating the day and he was a guest speaker. He was extremely anxious to impress upon me something which he felt particularly strongly about. He said that he was always happy for me to tell others about him and his story. He felt, however, that it was important that I ensured that the message which I conveyed should not be that we should all "… just thank our lucky stars" because "…here is someone far worse off than us." He reminded me that whenever I was speaking to audiences or working with groups in organisations, that I could not possibly know what "facts" the people with whom I was speaking had in their lives. Some could be far worse than Steve's.

The only thing that I can be sure of is that everyone has "facts" in their lives. Some will be good and some will be not so good. There will often be nothing we can do about those facts. We, therefore, have to make a choice. We have to make a choice of how we want our life to be and have the corresponding attitude accordingly – no matter what the facts are.

I don't know how many of you will remember a character on a TV comedy show called, "Unlucky Alf". Nothing ever went right for Alf. If he was standing at a bus stop waiting for a bus the bus would fly past him going through the puddle that he was standing next to and soaking him. In one particular sketch Alf is downstairs in his robe when there is a knock at his door. It's the postman. He gives him a letter from a well known football pools company. Inside is a cheque for a million pounds. Alf looks at the camera and says, "That's not like me." A minute later another knock at the door. A beautiful blonde neighbour has just come round to introduce herself. Alf gets into a panic. His world isn't like this. Nothing good ever happens to him. Then suddenly the picture on the TV screen goes wavy and fades in and out. When it comes properly into focus Alf finds himself in his bed fighting under his covers. He looks round, stares at the camera and says what he knew really to be true all along, "It was all a dream!" Suddenly the legs on his bed collapse, the bedroom floor collapses, and he falls through to his living room floor. There he is covered in dust, rubble and dirt – no longer a millionaire – no longer with the beautiful blonde neighbour. "That's better," he says. How many Unlucky Alfs do you know?

I'm just going to ask you to pause for a second before you read on. I suspect that if you were to take a little time out to reflect upon what you have just read most of you will probably be thinking that actually, what I have written so far is pretty much common sense, and that somewhere in your mind you already knew most, if not all of it. I think that's how I felt when I first came across the material behind this book. What I always struggled with, however, was the message that I seemed to get on how to make changes. We have already decided that it is extremely difficult to sustain any kind of change at a behavioural level only (leaf painting), and it is equally difficult to pull ourselves together, buck up, and just feel better when actually we feel lousy. I think the challenge that I always faced was that people told me (or I read) that what I needed to do in order to change the way I feel and ultimately, therefore, my behaviour, or the results I was getting, was to have a positive attitude!

Now I think that what you have read so far proves that all those writers and speakers who told me to be positive were absolutely right. It was the methodology (or perhaps my perception of the methodology) to actually "attaining" a positive attitude that was always my challenge. You see group hugging, "high-fiveing", massaging the shoulders of the person next to me, and looking in the mirror in the morning, smiling at the reflection, and telling it to "be positive", just didn't sit well with me. I think that part of the reason is that for me those kinds of methodology required me to force a change from the left to the right hand side of the tree in much the same way as I have mentioned for feelings and behaviour above. I think that maybe deep down I suspected that, and, therefore, needed to know and understand why it didn't end with attitude. The reality is that it doesn't. The fourth stage of this model – the roots which connect to and feed the trunk (your attitude) – is your beliefs.

CHAPTER 4 – "The 'Root' Cause"

I suppose that the first question which I need you to consider is just how many beliefs you were born with – 5? 10? 50? 100? The actual answer is of course – none. You do not come into this world with any pre-programmed beliefs. Psychologists tell us that we are born with two fears (which are probably the nearest things to beliefs). These are the fear of falling and the fear of loud noises. Both are apparently related to the birth experience! Please don't ask!! These are the only two "beliefs" you have in the first seconds that you are exposed to the world. Everything else you acquire – and that is something that we will explore in much more detail later. First, let's look at the tree again.

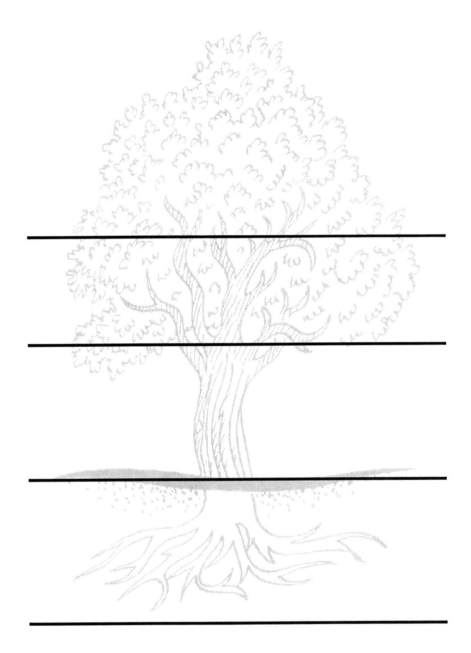

As before, fill in your words on the levels of behaviour, feelings, and attitude from your previous tree diagrams. Just as roots pass on nourishment to the trunk, so your beliefs about the facts in your life will determine your attitude to those facts.

We all have deep rooted beliefs. Your beliefs, which you would place on the right hand side of your tree, will inspire you. On the left hand side of the tree they will limit you (I suggest that you write the word "Inspirational" on the right of the tree at roots level and the word "Limiting" on the left).

It seems to me that from those very first seconds when we come into the world with our two fears and nothing else we start to build a wall. We build a wall between beliefs that will limit and beliefs that will inspire, and sadly all too often too many of us seem to build it from the left hand side. We build it from the perspective of limiting beliefs. Beliefs that say, "I just can't", "I'll never be able to do that", "It's just not who I am". Tragically sometimes we build a wall so high that we can't even see over to the other side let alone climb over.

Just take a moment now and think about yourself. What beliefs do you have about *you* right now? What beliefs do you have about you in your workplace, as a husband/wife/partner/parent/child/golfer or whatever else you do? How do the beliefs that you have about you affect your performance and your behaviour? How do they affect the 'you' that the outside world sees? Beliefs are mighty powerful tools to impact performance, good or bad. I want to see if I can build a couple of beliefs in you right now to affect your behaviour.

On the next page you will see a sentence. This is going to take some discipline, but please, at this stage keep the book open to this page without turning over.

The sentence is an ancient one rooted in the philosophies of people like Plato and Socrates. Many people cleverer than I am have said that to have an understanding, a true understanding of this sentence gives the answer, or the keys to improved performance.

What I am going to ask you to do in a minute is to turn the page and read this sentence through, just once, at normal reading pace. Once you have done that please immediately turn back to this page. It is very important that you only read it once. It should take no longer than 10 seconds, and then turn immediately back to this page. Please do it now.

Have you done it? What do you think? It's a complex sentence, yet a simple one. Not everyone understands its meaning fully the first time so again I'm going to ask you to turn the page and read it through once more at normal reading pace. This should take you no more than ten seconds. Once you have done this please move on to the next page of text.

FINE FOLKS ARE THE RESULT OF
YEARS OF GENETIC AND SCIENTIFIC
STUDY COMBINED WITH THE
EXPERIENCE OF MANY YEARS

Andrew O'Donoghue

Well? Does it mean anything to you? The answer is probably 'not'.

This time, however, I would like you to do exactly the same again. Turn the page over, read the sentence through, and again this should take no more than ten seconds, but this time I would like you to look at the sentence in a different way.

This time I would like you to count the number of times you see the letter "F" in that sentence. Please ensure that you take no longer than ten seconds and then again turn back to this page. Write down your answer in the space below.

How many F's were there? The vast majority of you, experience tells us, will have seen either two or three. Some may have seen four and some could have seen five. Some may even have seen six, and every now and then the odd person sees seven (that's the really "odd" person)!

The reality is that there are six F's in that sentence. Take another look. For those of you who still can't see six have a look for the ones sneakily hidden in the word *OF*. For those

56

who saw six initially you're probably wondering what the point of this exercise is. Some of you will, of course, have seen the sentence before. For those of you who saw two, three, or maybe even four, the answer will now be hitting you like a sledgehammer. Why does that happen?

We often skip the small words. I attempted to put you under pressure asking you to read the sentence quickly. Perhaps you were looking for meaning in the sentence – don't worry, it's totally meaningless! But the real answer comes actually from the power of the brain – the power of the brain to trick you and mislead you. When you just read the sentence though, you read it through twice not looking for the answer, and when you read the word *OF*, you read it phonetically as *OV*. This fantastically powerful brain of ours then immediately stores what we have read.

I asked you to read it again. Again the reading of the word *OF* is stored phonetically and your previous reading reinforced this. I then asked you how many letter F's there were in the sentence. The brain immediately sends you down the wrong path. It tells you that the word *OF* couldn't possibly have the letter F in it because you have already read it through twice and read it as a V.

In other words, I managed to do what I said I would do. I built a belief in you or rather, I helped you build a belief for yourself. And based on that belief you responded. Perhaps I could put it another way – based on that belief, you behaved. If you had not believed that there are two, three, four, five or six letter F's in that sentence, you would not have written the number that you wrote on the previous page.

I have another question to ask you now though. I wonder what would have happened if this book had then told you that the answer that you gave was correct. Let's say you'd written three F's and the book had gone on to say that there were indeed three F's in that sentence. What do you think you might have done had you been shown the sentence in the future and someone asked you how many F's there were? What would you have done? Would you have diligently read it through looking for the F's again? You may have done so, but experience tells me that this is usually not the case.

Quite often when we have seen something previously, we base our current answer on our first or past experience of that thing rather than taking a good look again. I wonder how many times you have come across that. How many times do people base answers to problems on their past experience rather than on the information that's in front of them? How often do people base their ability (or lack of it) to do something, upon their past ability (or inability)?

We see this all the time in organisations. We have worked with one organisation that had a vision to be "World Class". If you talked to the people in the organisation many had the belief that this was impossible. That belief always comes from past experience. I've been in to other organisations (including that one) where people have said to me, "You won't last. You're just flavour of the month. We've seen this kind of thing before. It's just a fad. It won't make any difference." And guess what......?

Or imagine you receive an organisation-wide e-mail from your manager or CEO. Have you ever heard people go down the, "Here we go again", route? "I was here the last time we received something like this. I know exactly what this means." And these statements are made by people who haven't even read the email? Think about it. And if you are the CEO I suggest you think about it even more!

On which side of the tree would you put those phrases if that is the belief that you have formed? What kind of attitude is that going to build in an individual?

Therefore, when an organisation asks us to work with its people following a strategic change initiative or a new systems implementation project, how do you think people quite often feel when they are asked to deal with the change? Perhaps they have used the system in a previous organisation where it was a failure. In cases like this the belief of those people (which then gets transmitted to others who have had no experience of the system) is that it didn't work before and so it won't work again. And ultimately, therefore, what happens? Does the initiative or system implementation succeed or fail?

The crucial point to understand here is that people behave not according to reality, but rather according to their *perception* of reality – or to put it another way, their belief about what's real. If you hadn't believed there were two, three, four, or however many F's you wrote down, you wouldn't have written the answer that you did – and so it is with most of the things that we do in life.

Ok, since that worked so well I would like to try again and build another belief in you. In a couple of pages you will see five black shapes (trust me there are five, not four, or three, or six!). I'm going to ask you to look for the shapes and I'm actually going to tell you what three of them are.

Andrew O'Donoghue

The first shape is an arrow pointing downwards. It's easy to spot. It's a small arrow and it's almost in the middle. In fact, I'll show it separately below.

The second shape to the left hand side some people say looks like a hat standing on end, maybe even Doc Holliday's hat out of one of the old western movies. Again I'll show it on its own below.

The third shape on the right hand side some people say looks like a Native North American Indian. And again to make this easier I will show the shape on its own on the next page.

Now I don't wish to put pressure on anyone, but at age seven my son was able to see those shapes and to do what I'm going to ask you to do next.

On the next page there will be two other shapes in between the three shapes you have already seen. I want you to look at those shapes and see if you can identify them. Different people may come up with different answers but take a look.

There is a common theme running through these shapes. Arrow – Doc Holliday's hat – Native American Indian. When you have had a look at the other two black shapes and have identified them I would like you to put the black shapes together.

When you put them together you will find that they make something. What I want to know is what do they make?

Why don't you have a bit of fun with this and try timing yourself.

Please turn the page over now.

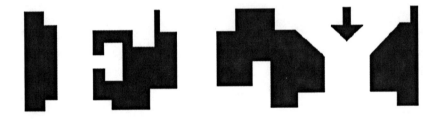

How did you do? How long did it take you? Are there some of you who still haven't seen it? Well, if so I will give you a clue.

When you put them together, the black shapes make an insect. Can you see it now?

For those of you who still can't see it I'll give you a bigger clue. They make a fly.

If you still can't see it then maybe you are focusing on the wrong thing. Instead of looking at the black shapes have a look at the spaces in between. What you are looking for is the word 'FLY' in the white spaces in between the shapes – FLY. See it now?

Obvious, isn't it? In fact I'll bet it's impossible now for you not to see it. I'll bet if you hold the page up to the light and look through the back of the page you will still be able to read it.

What happened in this case though? I fully accept that I led you up the garden path again. But perhaps more correctly, what I did was ask you to focus on the wrong thing. I asked you to focus on the black shapes when what you should have been doing was focusing on the spaces in between.

Think about it. Just how often does this happen in life? Think about the times that you see the potential in other people – maybe in your colleagues or team members, or your children, your husband, wife or partner, other people you work with, or your friends. It is all well and good you seeing potential in others, but unless and until those individuals can see the potential in themselves they won't be able to achieve the things that you believe them to be capable of – they will never be able to see the word 'FLY' because all they will be doing is focusing on the wrong thing.

The point here is that we all have limits – but so many of our limits have nothing to do with our genetic makeup. Many of our limits – the things we believe that we can or can't do – are *self-imposed!*

However, I now ask the sixty four thousand dollar question. How often do you do that? What do you focus on? If you focus on the things you don't want, the things you can't do, the problems that you face day in and day out, poor market conditions, lack of demand for your products, or poor economic climate, what result are you going to get? Your beliefs about who you are – what you can or can't do – ultimately determine your performance.

There is a wonderful little quotation often attributed to Henry Ford. However, I think it originally comes from the pen of Mark Twain. It says:

> "If you think you can or if you think you
> can't – you're probably right!"

Just write those words on your tree – 'can' on the right and 'can't' on the left. As you do that I'm going to ask you to think of the impact of beliefs on behaviour or results in the following examples.

The 6th May 1954 is a date in sporting legend. Some of you may recognise it straight away – but if you don't it doesn't matter. On 6th May 1954 Roger Bannister became the first person in history to record a sub four minute mile.

What I would like you to do is to think about the general consensus – the beliefs that people had on the 5th May 1954 about running a sub–four minute mile. I suppose it's obvious that most people probably thought it was impossible – and one of the main reasons that they would probably have given for their answer is that it hadn't been done before. I know you have all heard that one before. If you are anything like me, you will have seen or read many a business guru who has said that it is this kind of thinking that prohibits change and advancement in so many organisations.

Bannister was facing something more than that, however. He didn't just have the general consensus that a sub–four minute mile was unachievable; he had the experts telling him that it couldn't be done. The medical profession had publicly stated (at various times and in various ways) that it was physiologically impossible for a human being to run a sub–four minute mile. In other words if a human being ran a sub–four minute mile...they would die (now you can try that as a motivational tactic if you wish, but it is not one that you will hear me recommend!!). Hypotheses included (and I am paraphrasing and simplifying here) that:

> ➢ Your heart would explode because it could not cope with the speed at which it would have to pump blood around the body to ensure that oxygen got to where it was needed - or,

> ➢ Your lungs would implode as they could not cope much in the same way as the heart above - or,

> Too much blood would be required by the muscles, and therefore, insufficient supply (and therefore, oxygen) would reach the brain with the consequence that you would fall into a coma and die.

As I said – that's motivation! Imagine even if you were the world's greatest mile athlete in say 1952 and your coach, support team, family, and the public at large had great faith and belief in you. If you believed that you were going to die as a result of breaking this barrier, would you even attempt it?

What things do you not attempt to do – not because you think you are going to die, but just because you think you won't succeed? Just turn back to the opening sentence of this book and consider the first question I asked you now. Does that put things in a slightly different light?

Some of you will remember that Roger Bannister wasn't just 'Mr.' Roger Bannister, he became Dr. Roger Bannister. The people he ran with (Brasher and Chataway) were also medics. I recommend you read his book for the full story. Basically though, Bannister challenged the consensus – the beliefs of the time.

The world record for a mile at the time was just over 4 minutes 1 second. Bannister questioned the rationale that running just over 1 second faster was physically impossible. He also challenged why the physiological barrier was exactly 4 minutes. Why not 3 minutes 59 or 4 minutes 1? He reasoned that as time was an artificial measure devised by people, it made no logical sense to set a barrier at that exact mark.

On the 6th May 1954 he set out, therefore, to break the barrier and the record. And he did just that - 3 minutes 59.4 seconds.

I think that what happened subsequent to this is more fascinating and even more pertinent to the point which I am aiming to make. How long do you think it was before someone else managed to run a sub-four minute mile? How long before a second person was able to "do the (formerly) impossible"? The answer - just over a month by an Australian runner called John Landy.

But here's where it gets really interesting. In the 12-month period following Bannister's record breaking run, over 30 different athletes ran sub-four minute miles. And in the two year period following the run, over 300 different athletes achieved what had previously been impossible. In one race in Dublin in 1958 (dubbed the "Miracle Mile") the first five athletes across the line broke the 4 minute barrier. Imagine beating a barrier, that two years previously had been deemed "impossible," and still only coming fifth!!

Now that story illustrates what I think may be the single most important message of this book, and if you remember nothing else or take nothing else away from having read the book, then I ask that you take away and act upon this single point. You see -

The beliefs that you have in life, about anything, will ultimately determine your behaviour or performance or the results that you get in life - whether or not those beliefs are based on reality and fact.

Please just take a moment to re-read that sentence and make sure that you understand what I am saying. Your beliefs will determine your behaviour whether or not they are based on fact and reality.

Take the Bannister example. What I am saying is that it was not physiological fact or reality that stopped anyone achieving the sub-four minute mile before Bannister. It was simply that people believed it was either impossible or that you would die if you managed to succeed. The result was that for however many thousands of years we have been walking the Earth, no-one apparently achieved Bannister's feat until he did it on 6th May 1954.

I would now ask you to consider the above statement and apply it to you. I am going to ask you again a question that I posed a few pages ago. What beliefs do you currently have about you as:

> A leader, manager?
> An employee?
> A husband, wife or partner?
> A parent, son or daughter?
> A friend?
> A golfer, badminton player, swimmer or whatever other sport you take part in?

Consider your answers from both sides of the tree. Think of the things that you are good at first. Think of the things that come easily to you, that you do really well, consistently. Then think about the beliefs that you have about yourself in those situations. I can pretty much guarantee that they will be positive, if not inspirational.

Then think about the things that you don't do as well as you would like. In what areas would you like to see improvement? What things do you maybe consistently do wrong or you have often tried and just can't get the hang of? You should see a pattern start to emerge.

I have had many people, including a top World Golfer say to me, "The reason I have great self-belief is that I am really good at..." Well, take a look at the tree again. I would suggest that that is nothing other than...*results dependent thinking.* The challenge with that is that we might have to wait a long time to get the result we are waiting for. It would be awful if we could only have self-belief and a positive attitude when things are going well for us. The time we need self-belief most is when things aren't going well. Anyone can be positive in the good times!

If you stop and think for just a minute, every time someone achieves something for the first time, by definition the belief has to precede the result. It cannot be any other way, and yet all too often today I think we slip into the results dependent approach. How often do you hear a sports person interviewed on TV say something like, "All I need is one good win and everything will be alright"?

I remember running a session with Bolton Wanderers Football Club when they were in the old First Division (now The Championship). Although they had been playing well they had gone through a bit of a sticky patch at home drawing something like 5 consecutive games. (In two games - against Crystal Palace and Gillingham, I seem to remember they had been 3-1 ahead with about 15 minutes to go. Both games finished 3-3.)

I ran a session on the impact of beliefs on performance – which my colleague, Mike, and I had done several times before. One of the more senior members of the squad (whose name most people would recognise) stopped me and questioned me. He said that he had heard me/us speak so many times about beliefs (and the implication was that he was sick and fed up of hearing the same old thing). He asked me if I was suggesting that if they 100% believed that they would get promoted to the Premiership, that I would 100% guarantee that they would get promoted.

The answer of course was simple – "No". It doesn't work like that. But I did give him two guarantees (or as near as possible to guarantees) as follows:

1. In my opinion a 100% negative, limiting belief pretty much guarantees a 100% negative result. I can't think of any situation where, from a starting point of a 100% negative belief, I have achieved anything other than a negative result. I am not saying that this is impossible; I am just saying that I can't think of any situation where that has happened for me.

2. The second guarantee which I gave was that, in my opinion, a 100% positive inspirational belief gives me a 100% *best chance* of achieving the result that I want. I would suggest that to give ourselves the best chance of achieving something is all that any of us could ever really want or expect. (Incidentally, that season Bolton Wanderers did achieve promotion to the Premiership where, certainly up until going to press, they have not only remained ever since, but have improved year by year, with an outstanding manager in Sam Allardyce,

70

who has instilled in them exceptional levels of self-belief.)

Think of some of the amazing achievements throughout history and ask yourself whether any of them could have been achieved without the pre-requisite of self-belief. Without the belief in the first place I think you have to question whether these people would even have bothered to attempt the things that they finally achieved.

➢ Christopher Columbus setting sail to discover an alternative trade route to the East Indies by sailing around the world – a world which people at the time believed was flat

➢ Edison in his efforts (over 10,000) to discover "light without heat" – the forerunner of the electric light bulb

➢ Wilbur and Orville Wright achieving the first "powered flight"

➢ Walt Disney looking at a swamp in Florida and seeing the Magic Kingdom

➢ Neil Armstrong becoming the first man to set foot on the moon

So, my basic premise is that beliefs are the key – the cornerstone to any kind of success.

However, you need now to go back to the beginning of this chapter. What I said there was that none of us were born with any beliefs. If that's the case then, who or what gave us, gives us, helps us, formulate those beliefs? If we can answer that question fully we should have the key to permanent, sustainable, comfortable change and ultimately the ability to be at our best, as we define it, more often. The answer, however, is not quite as obvious as it may at first appear.

CHAPTER 5 – "It's the Thought That Counts"

I now need you to go through the exercise one more time. Write in all the words from your first four diagrams on the tree on the following page. Then in the soil, below the roots, write down the things and people that have influenced you in the formulation of your beliefs since the day that you were born. Take a minute to think about it.

You will probably have come up with some or all of the sources from the following list:

> ➤ Parents
> ➤ Teachers
> ➤ Friends
> ➤ Peers
> ➤ Leaders
> ➤ Managers
> ➤ The Government
> ➤ The Media
> ➤ Religion
> ➤ General Experiences

You may have more than, or variations upon, the above, but generally the above list is usually a fair representation of what people say.

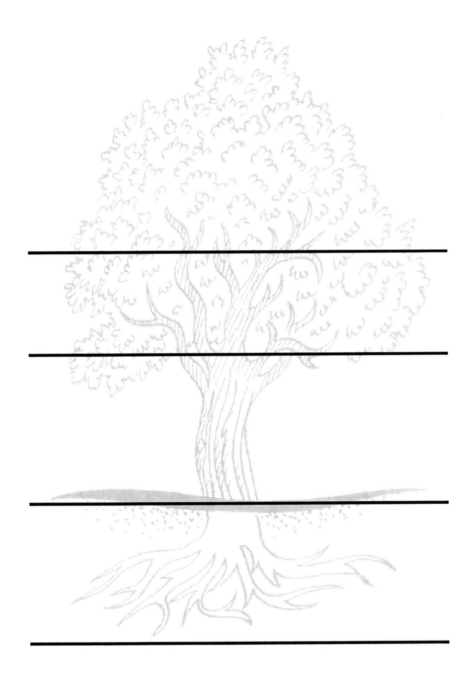

In his book, "*What to Say When You Talk to Yourself*", American Psychologist, Shad Helmstetter, relates how over the years he has asked the same two questions of various groups of people with which he has worked. The first is this:

"In the first 18 years of your life how many times did someone say to you, 'No'?"

Okay, when you have stopped laughing, what was the first number that came into your head? Thousands? Tens of thousands? Just to make you all feel better (particularly the parents among you), when I asked my son, Tom, the same question, his answer was "millions" (at the time he was only 13 so he still had another 5 years to go to be able to answer Helmstetter's question fully!). By the way, from his tone of voice he made it quite plain that about 90% plus of those "No's" had come from me – "Mr. Positive Attitude" – Dad!

The average figure Helmstetter compiled over the years was actually 148,000 'no's', which equates to over 22 per day (In my house it can be 22 a minute). He does however ask a second question: how many times in the same 18 years did someone sit down with you one to one and tell you how good you were and that in life you could achieve all the things you wanted to achieve? Answer? Well it was a little less than the 148,000 'no's'. The average answer Helmstetter received from his groups was between 3 and 4! Not per day; not per year; but 3 or 4 times during the entire 18 years!!!

I once had a delegate on a programme who put his head in his hands at this point – he had made the connection and seemed to think that in his case 99% of the "No's" had come from him. He said that he had three children, the eldest of which was a 17 year old daughter – and the two of them were consistently at loggerheads. He decided to go home that evening and in his words, "Sort it out". I was a little concerned since I was imagining the newspaper headlines the next day reading something like:

"17 Year Old Girl Strangles Father!!"

Anyway, when he came to the session the next day he related the previous night's events. He said he had gone home with the best of intentions. He had told his daughter that he loved her, that he wanted them to stop arguing all the time and that he was prepared to start doing things differently. In order to make changes, however, he needed to know exactly what it was that he did wrong. When he asked the question he said that his daughter immediately gave him the answer – "You always criticise me!" When he asked her to be a little more specific her reply was just as immediate – "You always criticise the way I dress!" He said that his own reply was equally as quick – "No I don't!" And then he remembered...

One Friday evening approximately eight months prior to the course, his daughter (then 16) had come downstairs wearing what he described as a "black handkerchief" in preparation for her Friday night out with the girls. He said that he took one look at her and said:

"You are not going out looking like a ....." (And I think I had better leave the final word to your imagination!)

He said he went hot and then cold as he thought of what he had, albeit in the heat of the moment, called his 16 year old daughter. He immediately apologised. One of the first things he said to her is something which I find fascinating and which caused me to stop and reflect. He said, "You know that's not what I think of you!"

How many times have I said that to people in my life – to colleagues, to people who work with me, to friends, to my wife and to my son? How many times?

One little phrase that we often use in our office is, "There's no such thing as a throw-away comment." The only person who can ever truly know what is meant by anything that is said is the person who is saying it. When we communicate something we are relying on our ability to make sure that others hear what we intend them to hear – and I think we all know that that is not always the case.

If you remember the little exercise that we did with the sentence containing the six F's, individuals' perceptions come into play when interpreting the meaning in any kind of communication.

A great example of this I think is when you give someone a genuine compliment. Just think about how different people respond to the simple (and let's assume for the purposes of this point "genuine") statement, "You look nice today!" What are the different kinds of responses that you could get to that one simple statement? Presumably the response you are looking for is "Thank you." However, what about:

> - "What do you want?"
> - "What have you done wrong?"
> - "What do you mean 'today'? Didn't I look nice yesterday?"
> - "What 'this old thing? I've had it for ages!"

Andrew O'Donoghue

I'm sure you could probably come up with a few more. Actually it is this point which will lead me to the most crucial part of this book which we will get to in just one minute. But first back to father and daughter.

After he recovered, the father then said that when he thought about it for a few seconds he couldn't actually remember criticising the way his daughter dressed on any other occasion – although he was honest enough to admit that he could have done so. When he said this to her and asked her on what other occasions he had criticised the way she looked, he said that the conversation ended as she stormed out in exasperation.

I would like you to just stop there for a moment and take a second to distil a couple of learning points from the story. The first one we have already covered. There really is no such thing as a throw-away comment.

The second point for me, however, is the crucial one to which I referred above. If you take a look at the conditioning words that you wrote in the soil at the bottom of the tree a couple of minutes ago, the chances are that you may have missed one. The one conditioning factor that most people miss is probably the most important one.

I don't think that I have mentioned anywhere else in this book the fact that before I started Advance Performance with Mike and Heather, for fifteen years I was a lawyer. I wasn't the greatest lawyer in the world but I was okay. Now I think I could put together a pretty good argument that would stand up in court to say that the conditioning factor that many people miss (and on courses that I run where we deal with this point, I would say that probably 99% plus of people do not think of this factor) is more important than the rest put together. I even think that I could put together a pretty good case to say that the conditioning factor that we have missed is in fact THE ONLY conditioning factor in our lives. Any guesses?

The biggest single conditioning factor
in your life is, in fact....YOU!

Everything else on the list – parents, teachers, leaders, media, etc. – is an external factor which you have to process or internalise. The mechanism that we use to process all our external conditioning is....THOUGHT. So the final two words that you probably want to write at the bottom of your tree are, "You" and "Thought" (or maybe "Think"). You may need to take a moment for that to sink in and register, and then I will take a few more minutes to explain exactly what I mean.

You see, we actually have absolute and total control over how we process every single external thing that we experience. When somebody tells us something we have a complete choice as to whether we believe them or not. We are in complete and absolute control of the way that we think.

When you read something in the newspapers it's up to each individual whether or not you believe what you read. The same applies to TV and to every single external piece of information that you come across, including, I suppose, the contents of this book.

I am not for one second suggesting that we have a conscious knowledge that we have this absolute choice. If you take a young child, for instance, he or she doesn't realise that

that there is complete freedom of choice about whether or not they believe in the jovial fat man with the white beard in the red suit who comes down our chimneys every year and gives us presents for nothing!! Children just believe this because they are conditioned to believe it from the earliest age by their parents. This is a wonderful thing. Anyone who has had children will always, I am sure, remember the look of wonder and astonishment at being told that Father Christmas "has been" and left the first bike or a new doll or a rocking horse or whatever else. As far as I am aware, no lasting damage is caused in the creation of this illusion by parents when children subsequently discover (often from an older brother or sister) that Santa Claus really doesn't exist (I hope I haven't just spoiled anyone's Christmas!).

However, if I am right and children do not realise that they have a choice as to whether or not they believe in Father Christmas perhaps there are other things that they are told, about which they don't realise they have a choice. How about:

> "You're lazy"
> "You're untidy"
> "You're clumsy"
> "You never listen"
> "If you don't work hard, you'll never get a job"
> "You're just like your father"

I'm sure that you could come up with lots more. Just think any one of the above through logically on your tree. Take the "untidy" example.

If we tell children that they are untidy, what do they think about whenever they are asked to tidy their rooms? What beliefs do they have about the state that their rooms are always in? What's their attitude to tidying their rooms? How do they feel when we tell them to tidy their rooms? And finally and most importantly, do their rooms ever get tidied? Probably 'Yes', but only when Mum does it!

We should remember that everyone is different. I do accept that in some cases a negative approach, e.g. "You'll never be able to do this", can produce an "I'll show you" response. In equally as many cases, however, I think that approach can just as easily produce a "You're right" response. It usually depends on the source of the conditioning and how the individual processes the information.

The same is equally true, of course, in a management sense when you look at motivational styles. What works for one may not work for others. There is no 'one size fits all' approach to motivation. I would strongly suggest that the positive approach tends on the whole to get more sustainable positive results than the negative. That, however, is a topic for a completely different book.

In the late 1990's a survey of over a thousand 11 year olds in the U.K. was taken asking them a series of questions, two of which were as follows:

1. What is your favourite TV programme?
2. What is your biggest fear?

In both cases the number one answer came from around 50% of those questioned. Now you are all probably racking your brains for U.K. TV programmes in the late 90's (incidentally, when a similar survey was undertaken in the late 60's the answer to Q.1 was "Dr. Who" and the answer to Q.2 was "The Daleks").

In all my time of relating this story I have only ever come across one person who got the first question correct and no one ever got the second one correct.

The answer to the first question (What was the favourite TV programme of a U.K. 11 year old in the late 90's?) was... The National Lottery Draw! Fascinating insight perhaps into how children were/are conditioned into thinking what is important in life. The answer to the second question (What was the biggest fear of an 11 year old in the U.K. in the late 90's?) is, I think, even more fascinating. The biggest fear according to the survey was...being murdered! Statistically I understand that there is no more chance of such a horrifying event occurring now than in the late 60's. I suppose the biggest difference is, when such an event does occur, the way it is today portrayed in the media.

An English University undertook a 10-year study looking at recession in the U.K. economy. The purpose of the study was to look at media portrayal of economic recession. The study concluded (amongst other things) that the greater the number of times that the word "recession" actually appeared in print throughout the ten years of the study, the deeper the actual recession that followed. I suppose it stands to reason that if people read something enough they start to believe it and ultimately behave in a recessionary way in terms of spending, saving, and investing.

It's really interesting, doing the job that I do, just how many times something happens, or I see something which immediately makes me think of the way that this model works.

In January (I think) 1998, I walked into the living room of our home around lunchtime. My son, Tom, was watching a sports programme, and Steve Coppell, who was manager of Crystal Palace Football Club at the time, was being interviewed. He was berating the fact that no matter what Palace did they just didn't seem to be able to win a game at home. This intrigued me. So the following day I bought a Sunday newspaper and decided to look into this for myself.

When I looked at the league table, Palace had played 22 games, ten at their home ground of Selhurst Park and twelve away from home. Of their ten home games they had lost six, drawn four, and won none – gaining a total of four points. This was indeed the worst record in the Premier League at that time. However, of their twelve away games they had won five, drawn four and lost only three – gaining a total of 19 points. At the time their away record was the best in the Premier League alongside Chelsea.

The story doesn't end there, however. The following season was our first working with Bolton Wanderers. I decided to relate the above story to the players linking the power of thought and belief to performance. I hadn't realised it at the time but one of the Bolton players had played for Palace the previous season. Firstly, he confirmed that everything that I said was correct (which is always a relief)! Secondly, however, he gave me two further pieces of information which I found even more fascinating.

He told me that in the '97/'98 season Crystal Palace actually won only three games at Selhurst Park. Two of the games were at the end of the season against Derby County and Sheffield Wednesday when their position was hopeless and they had already been relegated. The most interesting fact, however, was in respect of the other game that they won at Selhurst Park. The football fans amongst you may have already guessed what I am going to say. During the '97/'98 season (amongst others) Crystal Palace shared their ground with Wimbledon Football Club. The only other game that they won at Selhurst Park that season was their *away* fixture with Wimbledon!

As I said some time ago, however, I fully accept that most of us are not consciously aware that we are in control of how we process our conditioning. This does not make this fact any less real. It is a fact which we cannot change. There is also another fact that we cannot change. We cannot change our past conditioning. Every one of you reading this book is likely to be a product of 20, 30, 40 or more years of conditioning. I cannot change that. You cannot change that.

There are, however, two things that you can do about your conditioning. The first thing that you can do is to change how you now think about your past conditioning. Those of you who have seen Disney's, "*The Lion King*", may remember this little scene.

Rafiki, the wise old baboon, had gone looking for Simba to take him back to the Pride Lands and save his Pride. When Rafiki finds him Simba refuses to go. He says that he can't. He believes he is responsible for the death of his father and people won't understand. (Of course, it wasn't his fault, it was wicked Uncle Scar!) Rafiki looks at him and tells him that his father's death is in the past and he must put it behind him and move on. Simba says that he can't; people won't understand. Rafiki then takes the stick that he carries round with him and hits Simba on the head. Simba roars at Rafiki and asks why he did that. Rafiki looks at him and says, "It doesn't matter; it's in the past." Rafiki then takes another swipe at Simba, but this time Simba ducks and avoids the blow. Rafiki immediately looks at Simba and says (and I am paraphrasing here), "Ah ha! You can either learn from the past or run from it. On this occasion you chose to learn. Do so with other things." (Incidentally, see what other positive messages you can spot in Disney cartoons – they are full of them.)

The point is surely this: whatever we have said in the past or done in the past, we have said and done. We cannot change it; so let's not beat ourselves up over it. Absolutely learn from it so that we don't make the same mistake again, but once we have learned, move on.

The second thing that you can do (and perhaps this is even more important) is that you can change how you think about every single piece of conditioning with which you are confronted from...NOW!

If someone tells you that you are stupid, lazy, will never amount to anything, or if someone gives you any other negative conditioning, whether or not you accept that conditioning is a matter that is completely within your control.

When I was at school, I was pretty bright – not a genius by any means, but I used to do okay at most subjects. Maths

85

was never my favourite, but I never had any problem until I was 12 years old going into my second year of what is now High School in England (it was Grammar School for me, but I suppose that's just giving my age away again). Anyway, that year I got a new teacher for maths, and although I knew who he was, he had never taught me before. The school at the time was a very traditional "all boys" school – and this teacher was a very traditional, old–fashioned teacher. When returning homework, he used to stand at the front of the classroom, call out your name and throw your book back to you.

The first time he returned homework to the class in the first term of that school year, he went through the process that I outlined above – and the pile of books went down and down and still mine hadn't been returned. In fact, he got to the last three and I still didn't have my book. He returned two more and then finally I heard, "O'Donoghue?" I raised my hand. "Stand up boy." There was a stifled laugh from some of the class. "What do you call this?" as he opened my book to the homework page to reveal lots of red pen correction marks. More laughter. At this point he walked to my desk and said...."You may be good at other subjects but you will never be any good at mine!" At which point he tossed the book dismissively on my desk. The whole class erupted in laughter. That was to be the way I got my homework returned to me for the rest of the term.

In the maths exam at Christmas I achieved a result that I had never achieved before – I was bottom out of a class of thirty six. This then continued through to the Easter break when again I got the worst mark in the class in maths. Something else happened during the Easter break though – my teacher passed away. And before you jump to conclusions, I was three thousand miles away in the U.S. at the time!

When I returned after the Easter break, I discovered that for the final term I was to be taught by a teacher who had in fact taught me the previous year. At the end of the first lesson with him he asked me to stay behind, at which point he said to me, "What's going on?" When I pleaded ignorance at what he was talking about, he pressed me and asked why I was doing so poorly in maths. I looked at him and gave him the answer which was so blatantly obvious to me (and which at his age and with his experience should, so I thought, be obvious to him). My answer was a simple one. "I can't do maths, Sir!" At this point we had a discussion about the merits of my answer! When he asked me to justify why I couldn't do maths I gave him two reasons, both of which again seemed so obvious to me that I could understand why he even bothered asking me.

Reason number one – "Mr. 'X' said I was no good at maths" (forgive me, but I feel it's probably best if I don't print his name).

Reason number two – "Look at my results, Sir. They prove I can't do maths." I used my poor results as evidence of my inability to do maths, which seemed perfectly reasonable to me.

Now Mr. Starkie (and I'm very happy to print his name) wouldn't accept any of this. From that moment on he started adopting a different approach than the other teacher. He reminded me that in his class the previous year I had done pretty well and that this year should really be no different.

He used to constantly check that I understood what he was saying. When my homework was returned it came back to me with comments such as, "Well done", and "Getting better!"

And what was the result of all this, apart from the fact that I no longer dreaded maths? Well, in the summer end of year exam I came fourth – which I believe was my best result ever in maths.

One of my favourite quotations is by Eleanor Roosevelt who once said:

"No-one can insult you without your consent."

It is the same with conditioning. No one can condition you without your consent. The biggest piece of advice I can give you is to only ever accept conditioning which is designed to take you to the top right of your tree and to give conditioning to others which is designed to do the same. That doesn't mean that all criticism is bad and that the word "No" should never be used. All that I am saying is that sometimes perhaps we should redress the balance a little and that positive encouragement is a much better tool than negative reinforcement.

I didn't become more intelligent in my final term of my second year. I was fortunate to have a teacher who understood that the right way to get the best out of anyone was to help them build their own self-belief with a view to travelling up the right hand side of the tree. Thank you, Mr. Starkie!

CHAPTER 6 – Conclusion – "Miracle Gro™"

What I would like you to do now is to take a little time, reflect on what you have just read, and think for just one minute about the endless possibilities with which you are now faced.

Perhaps you could go right back to the first line in this book and think about the question I asked then – "What would you dare to attempt if you knew you were bound to succeed?" Please understand what I am saying here. I am not offering this book as a panacea. What I am doing is asking each and every one of you to challenge yourselves. What things are you not doing or achieving, not because you can't, *but simply because you think or say to yourself that you can't?*

I also think that this is the basis of an excellent leadership model. If as a manager or a leader you start with yourself, you should be able to see the impact that this could have in an organisational sense. Your thoughts about your business or company build your beliefs. These beliefs determine your attitude to the business, the economy, your market place, your competition, your own people/managers/leaders, etc. This attitude will dictate how you feel on a daily basis in all the work situations in which you find yourself. And the way that you feel will, of course, drive your own performance and behaviour.

The reason that I like this as a leadership model is that your behaviour and performance has the ability to impact and condition the people with whom you come into contact on a daily basis. It is my belief that at its most fundamental, leadership is nothing more than how one person's behaviour impacts another. The reality is, of course, that as leaders everything that you say and do impacts the people around you. That is why it is so important to start with yourself first, get your own behaviour 'right' before you start working on colleagues and team members.

Remember, I am not suggesting that you can defy the laws of physics with any of this. I am just asking you to take a step back and look at how the way you think affects the way you behave.

One of the things that we have done at my company, Advance Performance, is research the science and psychology behind why this process works. The material we have come across is startling. The model works not because of some psycho-babble, but is grounded in hard neuroscience. We have talked to neuroscientists, psychiatrists, psychologists, and doctors and have even delivered our programmes to members of their profession. I am currently considering a second book where I will go into the detail of that research – the science and psychology in support of why this cognitive model works.

For now, just take the model as it is. When they see this for the first time, the majority of people feel that it is simply common sense. I couldn't agree more. They also often say, however, that they like the logical steps that the model takes. I hope that you do too.

And now if I may I would like to finish with one final story.

Some years ago we were asked by a very good friend of mine, Martin, to work with some of his pupils in the High School at which he is head-teacher. I have to say at the outset that they were an outstanding group of young people when you got to know them, but they were the group in Martin's school for whom the system didn't seem to quite work. Typically their equivalents in previous years would leave school at 16 without sitting their GCE exams and, therefore, without any qualifications.

Martin had been on one of our programmes and asked if we would like to work with this group of young people. We agreed and my colleague, Mike, worked with them for about 18 months with me assisting him from time to time. The full story of the work is told in Mike's first book, "*they did; you can*", and so I won't tell it here.

However, whilst working with this group, Mike took them through this model of the tree and asked them at the end of the session what you should do if you had a tree with brown leaves that should really have green ones. If you recall earlier in the book I used the analogy of leaf painting as an unsatisfactory way to change behaviour. Well, Mike hadn't bargained for the fact that young Craig who was part of the group had just recently completed two weeks work experience in a Garden Centre! When Mike asked what you should do to get green leaves Craig shouted, "Put Miracle-Gro™ on it!" The class laughed, but Mike decided to play this one out. He asked Craig what 'Miracle-Gro™' was. Craig explained that it came as a liquid or in a sort of powder format that you could dilute and was a kind of plant food.

So Mike said, "Okay. So on my way home tonight I'll buy some 'Miracle-Gro™' for my tree and I'll rub it on the leaves." Well Craig proved that he had been listening by telling Mike in no uncertain terms that rubbing it on the leaves would be just like trying to paint the leaves and wouldn't work. "For 'Miracle-Gro' to work you have to pour it on the soil," Craig assured the group.

"Okay," Mike said. "So I'll buy some on my way home, pour it on the soil tonight, and tomorrow morning I'll have bright green healthy leaves." Again Craig looked at Mike with some disdain and told him that that wouldn't work either. "Why," asked Mike. "It'll take ages!" replied Craig. Before I upset the 'Miracle-Gro™' people, as good a product as it is, Craig was trying to make the point that it won't work overnight.

Then Mike said, "But that's no good to me Craig. I want green leaves tomorrow." To which Craig came out with the immortal line,

"Well, if you had wanted green leaves tomorrow, you should have thought of that months ago!"

If only Mike had had a video recorder! Change takes time - but it can only happen permanently, comfortably, and be sustained if we start from the soil.

So, I have one final question for you:

Is there anything in your life you would like to do differently?

Acknowledgements

Page viii   "Mountains and Molehills" written by Michael Finnigan and published by Authorhouse.

Page 29   Extract from the Bobby McFerrin song "Don't Worry, Be Happy", reproduced with kind permission of Fred Miller Original Artists.

Page 39   "Skippy the Bush Kangaroo", referenced with kind permission of Nine Network Australia PTY Ltd.

Page 44   "Behind the White Ball" written by Jimmy White and published by Hutchinson House, reproduced with kind permission.

Page 47   Unlucky Alf, a character from "The Fast Show", referenced with kind permission of the British Broadcasting Corporation.

Page 69   Bolton Wanderers and Sam Allardyce referenced with kind permission.

Page 75   "What to Say When You Talk to Yourself" written by Shad Helmstetter and published by Harper Collins, reproduced with kind permission.

Page 84   "The Lion King" copywrite the Walt Disney Corporation.

Page 89   "Miracle Gro™", with kind permission of The Scotts
           Company LLC.

To contact the author or for further information about
Advance Performance, email us at inspiration@advance.
tv or visit our website: www.advance.tv.

Printed in the United Kingdom
by Lightning Source UK Ltd.
127011UK00001B/333/A